MOTHER ESTELLE'S
EASY HOMEMADE

CANDY
COOKBOOK

COMPILED AND EDITED BY HILDA COOPER

ATHENEAN
P·R·E·S·S

LOOK FOR THESE FINE COOKBOOKS BY HILDA COOPER

FAMILY SECRETS: A SOUTHERN HERITAGE COOKBOOK

KIDS IN THE KITCHEN
A Cookbook of Yummy Foods That Kids Can Easily Prepare

HOLIDAY TRADITIONS: A SOUTHERN HERITAGE COOKBOOK

MOTHER ESTELLE'S OLD SOUTHERN RECIPE DESSERT COOKBOOK

THE ULTIMATE BROWNIE, BAR & COOKIE COOKBOOK

MOTHER ESTELLE'S EASY HOMEMADE CANDY COOKBOOK

MORE COOKBOOKS COMING IN 2002 FROM ATHENEAN PRESS

BRIDE'S GUIDE TO FAKING IT
A Cookbook And Marriage Survival Guide

HOW THE HECK DID I END UP IN THE KITCHEN COOKBOOK

SOUTHERN PLANTATION COOKBOOK

SHOO-FLY PIE & APPLE PAN DOWDY
Over 250 Old Southern Recipes That Are Nearly Gone With The Wind

ISBN 0-9701466-8-X

A Message from Hilda Cooper....

Candy making can be a very enjoyable experience, but there are a few things you should do to ensure you have the best success possible. First never make candy on a rainy day. Second, assemble all needed ingredients before you start; that way you won't have any surprises later. Third, always use the best ingredients you can afford. Finally, when making candy, you need to understand that **the secret to it all is in the *temperature*.** If you can afford to, invest in a good Candy making thermometer to insure the best possible results. If you do not have a thermometer, the cold water test is equally reliable.

CANDY-MAKING TEMPERATURE & COLD WATER TEST GUIDELINES

Thread begins at 230°F
   Makes a 2" thread when dropped from a spoon.

Soft Ball begins at 234°F
   A small amount dropped into chilled water forms a ball, but flattens when picked up.

Firm Ball begins at 244°F
   The ball will hold its shape and flatten only when pressed.

Hard Ball begins at 250°F
   The ball is more rigid, but still pliable.

Soft Crack begins at 270°F A small amount dropped into chilled water separates into threads that bend when picked up.

Hard Crack begins at 300°F
   Separates into threads that harden and are brittle.

Caramelized Sugar 310° to 338°F
   Between these temperatures, it will turn dark golden, but will turn black at 350°.

Try to make your candy on dry days. The candy does not set as well on humid or rainy days. Follow the recipes, watch the temperature of your candy and you should not have any trouble becoming a Master Candy Maker and Chocolatier.

Here are a few more related kitchen hints, to help you along:

If your bag or box of brown sugar turns hard as a rock, place a slice of fresh bread in the package of sugar and close securely. Let set for a few hours and your sugar will be as good as new! When measuring brown sugar, always pack it down!

To chill foods quickly put them in your freezer for 20 to 30 minutes rather than longer in the refrigerator.

A fresh egg's shell is rough and chalky looking. An old egg will have a shell that is smooth and shiny. To test, place the egg in a pot of cold, salted water. If the egg sinks, it is fresh. If it floats, it's not fresh, so throw it away! It is easier to separate eggs when still cold.

Always use a wooden spoon when making fudge.

To get the most juice out of fresh lemons, limes and oranges, bring them to room temperature and roll them under your palm against the kitchen counter before squeezing.

Measuring Corn Syrup, Molasses, and Honey: Dip measuring cup or spoon either in hot water or brush with oil before pouring in the syrup. This way, you get all that's in the cup to come out.

Vanilla: Make your own vanilla by placing 2 split and chopped vanilla beans in 1 liter of vodka or bourbon. Shaking the bottle once a day, let sit for 2-3 months, or until desired color. This also makes great holiday gifts when poured into glass bottles.

THE
RECIPES

AFTER DINNER MINTS

Ingredients:

| 3 | oz | Cream cheese | 1 | drop | Food coloring |
| 3 | cups | Confectioners' sugar | 1 | drop | Mint flavoring |

Beat cream cheese and add flavoring and food coloring. Mix in confectioners' sugar. Roll and knead well. Shape in small balls and flatten or put in flower molds. Can be made with different flavors and colors also. Vanilla, lemon, orange and almond are good choices.

ALMOND BRITTLE

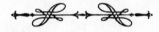

Ingredients:

| 2 | cups | Blanched almonds | 1 | cup | Butter |
| 1 | Tbs | Baking soda | 2 | cups | Sugar |

Combine butter and sugar in large heavy skillet or saucepan. Cook over medium-heat, stirring constantly to dissolve sugar. Stirring constantly, raise heat to medium–high and cook until mixture reaches the soft crack stage (280-290 °F). Stir in nuts and stirring frequently, continue cooking, to hard crack stage (300-310°F) or until a little of the mixture dropped in cold water forms a brittle thread which does not soften when removed from water.) Immediately remove from heat and sprinkle baking soda over mixture. Immediately pour mixture into large well-greased jellyroll pan. Cool for 30 minutes and then break into pieces.

ALMOND COCONUT BONBONS

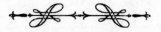

Ingredients:

14	oz	Sweetened condensed milk	1/2	cup	Almonds, chopped
			1/2	cup	Butter
2	lbs	Confectioners' sugar	5	cups	Coconut

Chocolate Coating:

8	oz	Semisweet chocolate chips	1	block	Paraffin
			1/4	cup	Shortening

Combine coconut, confectioners' sugar, milk, butter and almonds. Shape into patties. In top of double boiler, mix shortening, paraffin and chocolate over boiling water. Stir until chocolate mixture is completely blended. Using toothpicks or a fork, dip coconut patties into chocolate mixture, set on waxed paper until cool.

ALMOND HONEY DIVINITY

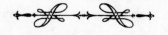

Ingredients:

3/4	cup	Chopped almonds	1/2	cup	Water
3	cups	Sugar	3	egg	Whites
1/2	cup	Honey	1/2	tsp	Almond extract

Whip egg whites until stiff peaks form. In a four-quart buttered saucepan, over medium heat, boil sugar, honey and water until syrup spins a thread (278°F). Gradually pour syrup over egg whites, continuously beating until slightly stiff. Beat in vanilla extract and nuts; drop with spoon on wax paper.

ALMOST HEAVEN NUT CANDY

Ingredients:

| 1 | cup | Pecans, chopped | 1 | cup | Brown sugar |
| 2 | large | Egg whites | | | |

Beat egg whites until stiff. Add nuts and sugar; pour into shallow pan greased with butter. Bake at 250°F until light brown. Cut into squares immediately after removing from oven.

ALMOND FUDGE

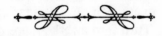

Ingredients:

1	oz	Blanched almonds, coarsely chopped	1/4	cup	Corn syrup
			2	Tbs	Butter
3	oz	Whipping cream	1/2	tsp	Salt
1/3	cup	Marshmallow crème	1-1/2	tsp	Almond extract
1-1/2	cup	Sugar			

Line a 9x9x2 inch pan with buttered foil, leaving a few inches to extend over each end. Butter sides of a 4-quart saucepan. Bring whipping cream to a boil over medium to high heat; remove from heat and add sugar. Stir continually until sugar dissolves and then add corn syrup, 2 tablespoons butter and salt. Return mixture to medium heat and bring to a boil, stirring occasionally to prevent scorching. Cook until the temperature reaches 238°F or until a drop from a spoon into ice water forms a soft ball.. Immediately remove from heat and set pan in the sink in one-half inch of cool water until mixture cools to 110°F. Beat in remaining ingredients until fudge begins to lose its gloss and become thick. Pour into prepared pan. As soon as the batch sets, remove from pan and place on wire cooling rack. When cold, store in plastic bag to age overnight before cutting into squares.

APPLE CANDY

Ingredients:

2	cups	Sweetened applesauce	1	Tbs	Cornstarch
2	Tbs	Unflavored gelatin	1/8	tsp	Salt
1/2	cup	Cold water	1	tsp	Apple pie spice
2/3	cup	Chopped walnuts	1	tsp	Lemon zest
1-1/3	cup	Confectioners' sugar	11-	Tbs	Lemon juice
1/3	cup	Sugar			

Soften gelatin in cold water. Pour applesauce into a 2-quart heavy saucepan. Cook until applesauce thickens and then add sugar, cornstarch and salt. Continue to cook over low heat, stirring constantly, until mixture is very thick. Stir in softened gelatin and then cook another two to three minutes until mixture begins to thicken again. Remove from heat. Stir in walnuts, apple pie spice, lemon peel, and lemon juice. Turn into an 8" square ungreased baking pan. Let stand 24 hours. Cut into squares. Roll in confectioners' sugar, and place on rack until outside of candy is dry. Store in covered container.

APPLE SPICED WALNUTS

Ingredients:

6	Tbs	Apple juice	1	Tbs	Apple pie spice
1/2	cup	Sugar	1	dash	Salt
1/2	cup	Light brown sugar	2	cups	Walnut halves

Butter a large baking sheet or pan and set aside. Combine everything but nuts in a large buttered saucepan over medium heat. Bring to a boil, stirring constantly, until the temperature reaches 236°F or until a drop from a spoon into ice water forms a soft ball.. Quickly stir in nuts and then spread onto a large buttered baking sheet, separating nuts as much as possible before they cool. When cool, store in covered container.

BANANA CHOCOLATE FUDGE

Ingredients:

2	med	Ripe banana, mashed	1	cup	Brown sugar
4	oz	Unsweetened chocolate, broken into pieces	3	cup	Sugar
			1-1/2	cup	Milk
4	Tbs	Light corn syrup	1/4	tsp	Salt
1	cup	Chopped pecans	6	Tbs	Butter
1	cup	Chopped pecans	1	tsp	Vanilla extract

Butter a 9x13x2 inch pan. Butter the sides and bottom of a 4-quart saucepan. In the saucepan, combine mashed bananas, chocolate, brown and Sugars, milk, salt and corn syrup. Stirring constantly, cook mixture over medium heat until the sugars dissolve and the mixture begins to boil. Continue to cook for about six minutes, stirring the mixture occasionally to prevent scorching, until the temperature reaches 236°F or until a drop from a spoon into ice water forms a soft ball. Remove from heat and without stirring, add butter. Allow the mixture to cool until lukewarm (about 110°F). Add vanilla extract and then beat until fudge starts to thicken and loses its gloss. Pour it into prepared pan. Sprinkle the fudge with chopped pecans, if desired. Gently press nuts into the fudge with a spatula. When fudge is cool and firm, cut the fudge into 60 pieces.

BILLIONAIRE SQUARES

Ingredients:

12	oz	Semisweet chocolate chips	1-1/2	cups	Pecans
60	each	Caramels	1	block	Paraffin
2-1/2	cups	Crispy rice cereal	1/4	cup	Shortening

Line a 9x13x2-inch with buttered wax paper. Unwrap caramels and place in a microwave bowl on high for one minute. Stir until caramels are melted. Microwave in additional fifteen second intervals, stirring after each interval, until caramels have completely melted. Do not overcook. Stir in crispy rice cereal and pecans and then press into prepared pan to an even thickness. Refrigerate for two hours. When chilled, cut into 1-1/2-inch squares. Melt chocolate chips and paraffin together in microwave safe bowl on high for one minute. Stir until fully melted, (microwave in additional 15 second intervals if necessary, stirring after each interval, but be careful not to overcook). Remove chilled caramel-squares from pan and, using a fork, dip in warmed chocolate coating. Return dipped candy to buttered foil to cool. Yields about 4 dozen squares.

BRAZIL NUT BARK

Ingredients:

12	oz	Semisweet	1	Tbs	Butter
		chocolate chips	1/2	cup	Seedless raisins
1	cup	Chopped Brazil nuts			

In the top of a double boiler, over simmering water, melt chocolate and butter. Remove from heat and stir until well blended. Stir in chopped Brazil nuts and raisins. Spread on buttered cookie sheet. Refrigerate for 2-3 hours, and then break into pieces. Store in covered container in refrigerator.

Alternate Microwave Method: In a microwaveable container, combine chocolate chips and shortening. Microwave on high for one and a half minutes. Stir until melted chips and shortening are completely blended Microwave on high in additional 15 second intervals if necessary to complete melting, stirring well between each interval.. Do not overcook. Stir in chopped Brazil nuts and raisins. Spread on buttered cookie sheet. Refrigerate for 2-3 hours, and then break into pieces. Refrigerate in covered container.

BRAZIL NUT PENUCHÉ

Ingredients:

1	cup	Ground Brazil nuts	1	cup	Milk
1	cup	Sliced Brazil nuts	1	tsp	Vanilla extract
3	cups	Brown sugar			

Butter a 9x13x2 inch pan. Spread sliced Brazil nuts evenly over the bottom. Set aside. Butter the sides and bottom of a 4-quart saucepan. In the saucepan, combine sugar and milk over low heat and stir until the sugar is melted. Increase to medium heat and bring to a boil, stirring occasionally to prevent scorching. Boil over medium heat until the temperature reaches 236°F or until a drop from a spoon into ice water forms a soft ball. Set the pan in the sink in about an inch of cold water, add vanilla extract and cool until lukewarm (about 110°F). Add ground Brazil nuts and stir until it begins to thicken and lose its shine. Pour into prepared pan in which the sliced Brazil nuts have been sprinkled. Cool and cut into squares.

BUCKEYES

Ingredients:

1-1/2	cup	Chunky peanut butter	1/2	cup	Butter
1	lb	Confectioners' sugar	1	Tbs	Vanilla extract

Chocolate Coating

8	oz	Semisweet	1	block	Paraffin
		chocolate chips	1/4	cup	Shortening

Beat together peanut butter, butter and vanilla. Gradually add confectioners' sugar. Roll into balls. In top of double boiler, combine shortening, paraffin and chocolate over boiling water. Still until well blended. Turn off heat and using toothpicks, dip balls into chocolate mixture, set on waxed paper to cool.

Alternate Microwave Method for Melting Chocolate: In a microwaveable container, combine chocolate chips, paraffin and shortening. Microwave on high for one and a half minutes. Stir until melted chips and shortening are completely blended. Microwave on high in additional 15 second intervals if necessary to complete melting, stirring well between each interval. Do not overcook. Proceed as above.

BUTTER CREAM BONBONS

Ingredients:
Centers:

| 2 | lbs | Confectioners' sugar | 1/4 | lb | Butter |
| 1/2 | lb | Cream cheese | 1/2 | tsp | Vanilla extract |

Chocolate Coating

| 8 | oz | Semisweet chocolate chips |
| 1/2 | block | Paraffin |

Cream cheese and butter together; add sugar and vanilla. Mix well until smooth. Store in refrigerator until firm. Roll into balls and coat with chocolate. Chocolate coating: In the top of a double boiler over simmering water, melt 1/2 block paraffin and 8 oz semisweet chocolate chips. Stir until smooth. Drop bonbons in chocolate remove with spoon and place on buttered wax paper. When dry, place in paper candy cups.

Alternate Microwave Method: In a microwaveable container, combine chocolate chips and paraffin. Microwave on high for one and a half minutes. Stir until melted chips and shortening are completely blended. Microwave on high in additional 15 second intervals if necessary to complete melting, stirring well between each interval. Do not overcook. Proceed as above.

BUTTER MINTS

Ingredients:

2/3	cup	Sweetened condensed milk	2-3	drops	Food coloring
			1/2	cup	Butter
7	cups	Confectioners' sugar	1	tsp	Salt
2-3	drops	Oil of peppermint	Decorator sugar if desired		

Cream butter and salt together until well blended. Add milk. Add sugar. Remove from bowl and knead until mixture is well blended. Add flavor and colorings. Divide candy in to several sections if desired to make several colors, if desired. Roll candies into small balls, dip in decorator or colored sugar if desired, and thin flatten slightly.

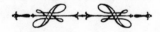

BUTTERSCOTCH CHOW MIEN CLUSTERS

Ingredients:

2	cups	Chow mien noodles	1/4	cup	Sugar
6	oz	Butterscotch chips	2	Tbs	Butter
1	cup	Cashew pieces	1/2	tsp	Vanilla extract
1/3	cup	Honey	1/8	tsp	Salt

Combine noodles and nuts in mixing bowl. In a heavy saucepan, combine honey, sugar, butter, vanilla and salt over moderate heat. Stirring constantly, bring mixture to a full boil. Remove from heat; add butterscotch morsels and stir until chips melt and mixture is smooth. Pour over noodles and nuts; mix gently until well coated. Quickly drop by heaping teaspoons onto waxed paper on baking sheet. Chill until firm.

BUTTERSCOTCH CRUNCH

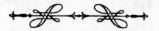

Ingredients:

2	cups	Mini or stick pretzels	1/2	cup	Salted peanuts
1	cup	Miniature marshmallows	3/4	cup	Sugar
			1/3	cup	Half and half
1	cup	Butterscotch chips	2	tsp	Butter

Combine pretzels, marshmallows and peanuts in a large bowl; set aside. Combine sugar, half and half and butter in a heavy saucepan over medium heat. Stirring constantly, bring to a boil. Add butterscotch chips and let stand for one minute to soften pieces; then stir until well combined. Cook for another 5 minutes, undisturbed. Remove from heat. Pour butterscotch mixture over pretzel mixture. Toss until everything is well coated. Quickly drop by rounded spoonfuls on baking sheets lined with wax paper. Chill until firm. Store in tightly covered container

BUTTERSCOTCH DROPS

Ingredients:

2	cups	Sugar	2	Tbs	Water
1/4	cup	Light corn syrup	2	Tbs	Vinegar
1/2	cup	Butter			

Combine all ingredients in heavy 2-quart saucepan. Stir and cook over medium heat until sugar is dissolved. Reduce heat and cook at a medium boil, stirring as mixture thickens. If sugar crystals form on sides, wipe off with wet pastry brush. Cook to hard crack stage, 300°F. Remove from heat and let stand 1 minute. Meanwhile, butter 2 sheets of foil and place on 2 baking sheets. Quickly drop spoonfuls of butterscotch onto foil, making patties about 1" in diameter. Space 1/2" apart. When cool, wrap in wax paper and store in covered container.

CANDY ORANGE SLICES

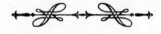

Ingredients:

1-3/4	oz	Dry fruit pectin	1	cup	Light corn syrup
3/4	cup	Water	2	tsp	Orange extract
1/2	tsp	Baking soda	2-4	drops	Orange food color
1	cup	Sugar	1/2	tsp	Citric acid

Sugar for dusting candy molds.

Lightly grease candy molds, sprinkle with sugar. In small saucepan, combine fruit pectin, water and baking soda; set aside. In a large saucepan pan, combine sugar and corn syrup, Place both saucepans over moderate heat, stirring alternately until foam subsides in the soda mixture, about 5 minutes. Pour pectin mixture in a slow, steady stream into the boiling sugar mixture, and stirring constantly, boil for one minute more. Remove from heat and stir in flavoring, food color and citric acid. Pour into prepared molds. Let set for 24 hours. Remove from molds and allow to age at least a day before storing in container.

CANDIED TOASTED PECANS

Ingredients:

1/2	cup	Light corn syrup	2	Tbs	Butter
1/3	cup	Light brown sugar	1/2	tsp	Vanilla extract
3	cups	Pecan halves	1/3	cup	Sugar

Toast pecans in 13x9x2-inch baking pan in preheated oven at 250°F for 5 minutes. Melt butter in 2-quart saucepan over medium heat; stir in corn syrup, vanilla and brown sugar. Stirring constantly, bring to a boil; boil without stirring exactly 5 minutes. Pour syrup over nuts, stirring constantly to coat evenly. Bake an additional one hour, stirring several times. Remove from oven, and sprinkle nuts with Sugar, tossing to coat evenly; immediately spread out on greased cookie sheets to cool. Quickly separate into individual pecan halves; cool. Store in tightly covered container.

CAPPUCCINO TRUFFLES

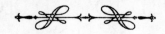

Ingredients:

2	Tbs	Instant coffee powder	2	Tbs	Brandy flavoring
3	cup	Crushed chocolate wafers 7	1	cup	Chopped pecans
	oz	Marshmallow crème	2	Tbs	Orange peel
2	Tbs	Orange juice			

Coatings:

2	Tbs	Cocoa	1/2	cup	Coconut to coat
2	Tbs	Confectioners' sugar			

Dissolve coffee in a measuring cup with combined juice and flavorings. Place marshmallow crème in a large mixing bowl and gradually beat in coffee mixture. Stir in crushed chocolate wafers, pecans and orange peel. Shape into 1-1/4 inch balls. Roll half of the balls in combined cocoa and confectioners' sugar. Roll remaining balls in coconut. Makes about 5 dozen.

CARAMEL POPCORN

Ingredients:

3	quarts	Popcorn, popped	1/2	cup	Butter
3	cups	Mixed nuts	1/2	tsp	Salt
1	cup	Brown sugar	1/2	tsp	Baking soda
1/2	cup	Light corn syrup	1/2	tsp	Vanilla extract

Preheat oven to 250ºF. In a large roasting pan combine the popcorn and nuts, place in oven to warm. Combine brown sugar, corn syrup, butter and salt in a saucepan over medium heat. Bring to a boil, stirring constantly, then boil for 4 minutes without stirring. Remove from heat; stir in baking soda and vanilla, and immediately pour over the warm popcorn and nuts, tossing to coat well. Bake popcorn mixture an hour at 250ºF, stirring ever 15 minutes. Cool and break apart. Store in an airtight container. Makes 4 quarts.

CARNIVAL PISTACHIO BALLS

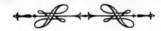

Ingredients:

16	oz	Confectioners' sugar	1/3	cup	Light cream
1	small	Box instant pistachio pudding mix	1/4	cup	Butter, softened

Coating:
3/4   cups   Chopped pistachios, decorator candies or sugars

Combine confectioners' sugar and pistachio pudding mix. Add cream and butter. Knead until ingredients are thoroughly mixed. Shape mixture into 1-inch balls. Roll in chopped nuts, jimmies or colored sugar as desired. Store in refrigerator. Makes 2-1/2 dozen.

CARROT WALNUT CREAM FUDGE

Ingredients:

3	cups	Peeled and grated young carrots	7	cups	Sugar
			1	cup	Water
14	oz	Sweetened condensed milk	2	tsp	Lemon extract
			1	cup	Chopped walnuts

Butter 9x13x2 inch pan and butter upper sides of an 8-quart heavy stockpot. Combine all ingredients except lemon extract and nuts in the stockpot over low heat and stir until the sugar is melted. Increase to medium heat and bring to a boil, stirring occasionally to prevent scorching. Boil over medium heat until the temperature reaches 236°F or until a drop from a spoon into ice water forms a soft ball. Set the pan in the sink in about an inch of cold water, add vanilla extract and cool until lukewarm (110°F). Remove from sink and beat until fudge begins to thicken and lose its gloss. Quickly stir in nuts and pour into prepared pan. Allow to firm but not harden before cutting into squares

CASHEW BRITTLE

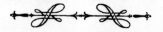

Ingredients:

2	cups	Sugar	1/2	cup	Water
1	cup	Light corn syrup	3	cups	Cashew halves
1	cup	Butter	1-1/2	tsp	Baking soda

Butter two large baking sheets and set aside. Combine sugar, corn syrup, butter and water in a large heavy saucepan. Cook over medium-heat, stirring constantly to dissolve sugar. Stirring constantly, raise heat to medium–high and cook until mixture reaches the soft crack stage (280-290°F). Stir in nuts and continue stirring frequently, cooking, until mixture reaches the hard crack stage (300-310°F) or until a little of the mixture dropped in cold water forms a brittle thread which does not soften when removed from water.) Immediately remove from heat and sprinkle baking soda over mixture. Quickly pour mixture onto large well-greased baking sheets. Cool completely and then break candy into pieces. Store in a tightly covered container.

CASHEW CARAMEL FUDGE

Ingredients:

2-1/2	cups	Sugar	1/3	cup	Butter
12	oz	Semisweet chocolate chips	5	oz	Evaporated milk
			3/4	cup	Cashews
7	oz	Marshmallow crème	1	tsp	Vanilla extract
24	each	Caramels, quartered			

Line a 9-inch square baking pan with foil; butter the foil with 2 teaspoons butter. Set aside. In a large heavy saucepan, combine milk, sugar and remaining butter. Cook over medium heat, stirring continuously, until sugar is dissolved. Bring to a rapid boil; boil for 5 minutes, stirring constantly. Remove from the heat; stir in chocolate chips and marshmallow crème until melted. Fold in caramels, cashews and vanilla extract; mix well. Pour into prepared pan. Cool. Remove from pan and cut into 1-inch squares. Store at room temperature. Yields about 3 pounds.

CHARLESTON BENNE (SESAME) SEED BRITTLE

Ingredients:

2	cups	Sugar	2	cups	Sesame seeds
1/2	tsp	Vanilla extract	1	tsp	Baking soda
1/2	tsp	Lemon extract			

Toast sesame seeds. Set aside. Combine the extracts and sugar in a heavy skillet or saucepan. Cook over medium-heat, stirring constantly to dissolve sugar. Stirring constantly, raise heat to medium–high and cook until mixture reaches the soft crack stage (280-290°F). Stir in seeds and continue stirring frequently, cooking until mixture reaches the hard crack stage (300-310°F) or until a little of the mixture dropped in cold water forms a brittle thread which does not soften when removed from water.) Immediately remove from heat and sprinkle baking soda over mixture. Quickly pour mixture onto large well-greased baking sheets. Cool completely and then break candy into pieces. Store in a tightly covered container.

CHERRY CREAM GELS

Ingredients

1/2	cup	Maraschino Cherries, chopped	12	oz	Cherry gelatin
			1/2	tsp	Almond extract
3	oz	Vanilla pudding mix	1	cup	Cold milk
2-1/2	cups	Boiling water			

Dissolve gelatin in boiling water, stirring at least 3 minutes until completely dissolved. Cool 30 minutes at room temperature. In a separate bowl, beat together milk, almond extract and pudding mix. Quickly pour pudding and chopped cherries into gelatin and whisk together until well blended. Pour into 13x9-inch pan. Refrigerate overnight. When firmly set, cut into small squares or decorative shapes. Keep refrigerated in a covered container.

CHERRY WALNUT DIVINITY

Ingredients:

1	cup	Chopped walnuts	2	large	Egg whites
1	cup	Candied cherries	1/8	tsp	Salt
3	cups	Light brown sugar	1	tsp	Vanilla extract
1	cup	Water	1	cup	Corn syrup

Boil sugar, syrup, salt and water to firm ball stage (248° F). Pour syrup slowly over stiffly beaten egg whites, beating constantly. Beat until candy begins to stiffen. Add chopped candied cherries, flavoring, and nuts. Drop by spoonfuls onto waxed paper.

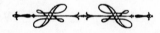

CHOCOLATE WALNUT PUFFS

Ingredients

6	oz	Semisweet chocolate chips	1/2	tsp	Vanilla
			1/2	tsp	Vinegar
2	large	Egg whites	3/4	cups	Chopped nuts
1/2	cup	Sugar	1	dash	Salt

Melt chocolate chips in a microwaveable bowl on high for one minute. Stir to melt. Microwave in additional 15 second intervals if necessary. DO not over cook. Beat egg whites until foamy. Add dash of salt. Gradually add sugar and beat until glossy stiff peaks form. Add vanilla and vinegar. Fold in chocolate chips and nuts. Drop by tsp on greased cookie sheet. Decorate with nut halves, if desired. Bake in 350ºF oven for 10-12 minutes remove immediately.

CHOCOLATE WALNUT RUM BALLS

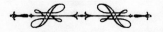

Ingredients:

1	cup	Walnuts, finely chopped	4	Tbs Rum
2	cup	Grated German chocolate	1/4	cup Cocoa powder
1-1/2	cup	Confectioner's sugar		

Combine nuts, sugar, and chocolate. Microwave for just 30 seconds. Add rum to form a stiff dough. Form into one inch balls and roll in cocoa to coat.

CHOCOHOLIC BARK

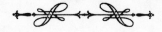

Ingredients:

12	oz	Semisweet chocolate chips	2	cups	Pecans, chopped
12	oz	Milk chocolate chips	12	oz	White chocolate chips
2	Tbs	Solid shortening	1/2	cup	Crushed toffee bars
1	block	Paraffin	1	cup	Candy coated chocolate pieces

Line a large cookie sheet with buttered wax paper or aluminum foil. Combine semisweet chocolate, milk chocolate, paraffin, and solid shortening in a large microwaveable bowl and microwave on high for one minute. Remove and stir. Repeat in additional 15 second intervals on high followed by vigorous stirring each time, as necessary until chocolate and paraffin have melted enough to blend thoroughly when stirred. Set aside to cool for 10 minutes, and then stir in nuts, then candy coated chocolate pieces, and then white chocolate. Quickly pour mixture onto prepared cookie sheet Spread to the desired thickness. Refrigerate for one hour. Peel away the foil or wax paper and break into pieces.

CHOCOLATE CHOW MIEN CANDY CLUSTERS

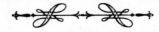

Ingredients:

1/2	block	Paraffin	3	oz	Chow mien noodles
12	oz	Semisweet chocolate chips	2	cups	Cocktail peanuts

Melt Semisweet chocolate chips and paraffin in top of double boiler. Stir until well blended. Remove from heat and immediately stir in chow mien noodles until well coated and then stir in peanuts. Drop mounded spoonfuls on buttered wax paper. Let cool until firm. Makes about two-dozen candies. Store in covered container.

CHOCOLATE COATED CHEX® MIX

Ingredients:

4	cups	Corn Chex®	4	cups	Miniature pretzels
4	cups	Wheat Chex®	4	cups	Mixed nuts

Dark Chocolate Coating:
12	oz	Semisweet chocolate chips	1/3	cups	Solid shortening

White Chocolate Coating:
12	oz	White chocolate chips	1/3	cups	Solid shortening

Powdered sugar for dusting

Combine pretzels, cereal and mixed nuts in bowl and thoroughly mix. Divide mix evenly into two bowls; set aside. Set aside. Put the chocolate chips and shortening in a microwaveable bowl and microwave on high for 1 minute. Stir until melted. Microwave an additional 15 second intervals if needed to complete melting. Do not overcook. Repeat with white chocolate coating. Pour white chocolate over one bowl of cereal mix and dark chocolate over the other. Stir until all pieces are evenly coated then pour coated cereal into large plastic bag with powdered sugar. Seal and shake until all the pieces are well coated. Spread on waxed paper to cool. Serve separately, or combine both into one large bowl to serve.

CHOCOLATE COVERED CHERRIES

Ingredients:

3	lb	Confectioners' sugar	8	tsp	Melted butter
30	oz	Maraschino cherries	6	tsp	Light corn syrup
14	oz.	Sweetened condensed milk	1	tsp	Almond extract

Coating:

12	oz	Semisweet chocolate chips	1/2	Tbs	Solid shortening
			1/2	block	Paraffin wax

In a large mixing bowl, combine butter, corn syrup, sweetened condensed milk, vanilla, and sugar. Knead into pliable dough. Wrap dough around maraschino cherry and form into a ball. The balls should be approximately the size of walnuts with a cherry in the center. Place a toothpick or small wooden skewer in each ball and place in freezer to chill until firm. Meanwhile, in a double boiler over simmering water, melt chocolate chips, paraffin and shortening together. Dip the chilled balls in the chocolate, and then place on parchment paper to cool and set. Store several days for clear syrup to develop inside.

Alternate Microwave Method for Chocolate Coating: In a microwaveable container, combine chocolate chips paraffin and shortening. Microwave on high for one and a half minutes. Stir until melted chips and shortening are completely blended. Microwave on high in additional 15 second intervals if necessary to complete melting. Do not overcook. Proceed as above.

CHOCOLATE COVERED CHERRY FUDGE

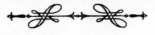

Ingredients:

1	can	Sweetened condensed milk	12	oz	Semisweet chocolate chips
1/2	cup	Maraschino cherries	3	oz	Cherry gelatin
1/2	cup	Chopped pecans	1	tsp	Almond extract

Maraschino cherry halves for decoration (optional)

Line 8-inch square pan with foil. In medium-size microwave-safe bowl combine sweetened condensed milk, cherry gelatin and chocolate chips; stir lightly. Microwave at HIGH for 1-1/2 to 2 minutes or until chips are melted and mixture is smooth when stirred. Stir in almonds, cherries and almond extract. Spread evenly in prepared pan. Garnish with cherry halves, if desired. Cover; chill until firm. Cut into 1-inch squares. Cover; store in refrigerator.

CHOCOLATE COVERED PECAN DIVINITY

Ingredients:

7	oz	Marshmallow crème	2	cups	Sugar
1	tsp	Vanilla extract	1/2	cup	Water
1	cup	Chopped pecans	1/8	tsp	Salt

Coating:

| 12 | oz | Semisweet chocolate chips | 1/2 | Tbs | Solid shortening |
| | | | 1/2 | block | Paraffin wax |

Boil sugar, water and salt in saucepan until mixture forms a hard ball in cold water (or 252°F on candy thermometer). Place marshmallow crème in large bowl; whisk in hot syrup in slow steady stream. Continue stirring until slightly stiff. Add vanilla extract and nuts (or cherries). Drop by spoonful onto wax paper and allow to thoroughly dry. Then insert a toothpick in each piece and freeze for at least one hour. In a microwaveable container, combine chocolate chips paraffin and shortening. Microwave on high for one and a half minutes. Stir until melted chips and shortening are completely blended. Microwave on high in additional 15 second intervals if necessary to complete melting. Do not overcook. Dip the chilled divinity in the chocolate, and then place on parchment paper to cool and set.

CHOCOLATE COVERED PEANUT BUTTER FUDGE

Ingredients:

1/4	cup	Whipping cream	3/4	cup	Peanut butter
2	cup	Sugar	12	oz	Semisweet chocolate chips
1/2	cup	Evaporated milk			
1	Tbs	Butter			

Butter an 8x8x1/2-inch pan. Butter the sides of a 4-quart saucepan. Combine the sugar, evaporated milk and butter in saucepan, and while stirring continuously, bring to a boil over medium heat. Remove from heat after mixture has boiled for one minute and beat in peanut butter. Pour fudge into prepared pan. Meanwhile, melt the chocolate chips in a microwaveable bowl on high for one minute, stir until melted, and then stir in the cream. Pour chocolate mixture over the peanut butter fudge. Allow to set and then cut into squares. Store in covered container.

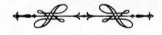

CHOCOLATE MACAROON TURTLES

Ingredients

7	oz	Almond paste	2	large	Egg whites
1/2	cup	Cocoa	2	cups	Pecan halves
1/4	cup	Sugar			

Preheat oven to 400°F. Combine all of the ingredients, except for the pecans, until thoroughly mixed and smooth. Place the mixture into a zip-top plastic bag. Arrange sets of 5 pecans on a baking sheet in a star patterns to form the head and legs of the turtle. Cut off a 1-inch piece from the corner of the plastic bag. Pipe the mixture into the centers of the pecan clusters to form the shells of the turtles. Bake at about 15 minutes until the shells begins to crack and set.

CHOCOLATE MACADAMIA NUT BRITTLE

Ingredients:

1-1/2	cups	Semisweet chocolate chips	1	cup	Butter
			1-1/2	cups	Sugar
2	cups	Macadamia nuts	1	Tbs	Baking soda
4	Tbs	Light corn syrup			

Coarsely chop macadamia nuts and then set aside. Line bottom and sides of 9x13x2-inch pan with aluminum foil. Butter foil generously. Combine butter, sugar, and corn syrup in a large heavy saucepan. Cook over medium-heat, stirring constantly to dissolve sugar. Raise heat to medium–high and, stirring constantly, cook until mixture reaches the soft crack stage (280-290°F). Stir in chopped nuts and continue cooking, stirring frequently, until mixture reaches the hard crack stage (300-310°F) or until a little of the mixture dropped in cold water forms a brittle thread which does not soften when removed from water. Immediately remove from heat and sprinkle baking soda over mixture. Quickly pour mixture into prepared pan and spread evenly. Sprinkle with chocolate chips; let chips melt and then spread evenly over top. Cool 30 minutes to an hour in freezer. Remove candy from freezer and remove from pan. Peel off foil and break into pieces.

CHOCOLATE MARSHMALLOW CREAM CHEESE FUDGE

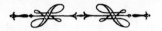

Ingredients:

1	cup	Semisweet chocolate chips	1	dash	Salt
			3	oz	Cream cheese
2	cups	Confectioners' sugar	1	tsp	Vanilla extract
1	cup	Miniature marshmallows	1	tsp	Cream

In a large mixing bowl, beat cream cheese until soft and smooth. Gradually add confectioners' sugar until well blended. Melt chocolate chips in microwaveable bowl on high for one-minute. Stir until melted. Microwave another 20 seconds if necessary. Add vanilla extract and cream; mix until thoroughly blended. Beat melted chocolate mixture into cream cheese mixture. Fold in marshmallows, and place in buttered 8-inch square pan. Place in refrigerator until firm and then cut into squares.

CHOCOLATE NUT COVERED MARSHMALLOWS

Ingredients:

2	cup	Milk chocolate chips	7	oz	Marshmallow crème
14	oz	Sweetened condensed milk	40	large	Marshmallows
			4	cups	Chopped pecans

In a microwave or heavy saucepan, heat chocolate chips, sweetened condensed milk and marshmallows crème just until melted; stir until smooth (mixture will be thick). With tongs, immediately dip marshmallows, one at a time, in chocolate mixture. Shake off excess chocolate; quickly roll in pecans. Place on wax paper-lined baking sheets. (Reheat chocolate mixture as necessary for easier coating.) Refrigerate until firm. Store in the refrigerator in an airtight container. Yields 40.

CHOCOLATE-PEANUT BUTTERCANDY APPLES

Ingredients:

12	each	Wooden sticks	12	med	Apples
10	oz	Peanut butter chips	1/2	cup	Solid shortening
12	oz	Semisweet chocolate chips	1	cup	Chopped peanuts

Wash and dry each apple. Insert a wooden stick into each apple. Line a large pan or tray with waxed paper. In medium microwave-safe bowl, stir together peanut butter chips and shortening. Microwave on high (100%) for 1-1/2 minutes or until chips are softened. Stir until melted. If necessary after stirring to further melt chips, microwave on high an additional 15 seconds. Stir until thoroughly blended. Dip apples in mixture. While removing the apple from the mixture, twirl to remove excess coating. Set aside on wax paper to harden. In a separate medium microwave-safe bowl, stir together chocolate chips and shortening. Microwave on high (100%) for 1-1/2 minutes or until chips are softened. Stir until melted. If necessary after stirring to further melt chips, microwave on high an additional 15 seconds. Stir until thoroughly blended. Dip peanut butter coated apples in mixture. While removing the apple from the mixture, twirl to remove excess coating. Dip lower half of chocolate coated apple in chopped peanuts if desired. Allow to cool on prepared wax paper lined tray. Refrigerate until used.

CHOCOLATE PEANUT BUTTER MARSHMALLOW PUFFS

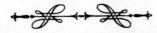

Ingredients:

2	cups	Semisweet chocolate chips	1/2	cup	Peanut butter
			1/2	cups	Chopped peanuts
3	Tbs	Shortening	36	large	Marshmallows

Line a 9-inch square pan with buttered foil, allowing foil to extend over the edge of pan. Arrange marshmallows in pan, in six rows each direction. In a microwave-safe bowl, melt chocolate chips, peanut butter and butter on HIGH for 1 to 3 minutes until chips are shiny and beginning to melt. Remove and stir until mixture is thoroughly melted and blended. Quickly pour chocolate over marshmallows; sprinkle with chopped peanuts. Chill completely. Lift foil from pan, cut between marshmallows. Makes 36 candies.

CHOCOLATE PECAN FUDGE

Ingredients:

3/4	cup	Cream	1-1/2	cups	Pecans, chopped
3	cups	Sugar	1/2	Tbs	Salt
1/2	cup	Light corn syrup	1/4	cup	Butter
6	oz	Unsweetened chocolate	1	Tbs	Vanilla extract
3/4	cup	Milk			

In a heavy 3-quart saucepan, cook milk, cream and chocolate, stirring constantly until chocolate melts and mixture is smooth. Blend in sugar, syrup, and salt, stirring until sugar dissolves. Cook until candy thermometer registers 236°F. Remove from heat and add butter and vanilla. Set saucepan in cold water and cool mixture to 110° without stirring, then beat vigorously until candy begins to lose its gloss and starts to hold its shape. Pour into a buttered 9-inch square pan and spread quickly into an even layer. Cool and then cut into squares. Makes 40 pieces.

CHOCOLATE PUDDING FUDGE

Ingredients:

1	small	Box chocolate pudding mix (NOT instant)	1	cup	Sugar
3/4	cup	Chopped pecans or walnuts	1/2	cup	Brown sugar
			1	Tbs	Butter
1/2	cup	Evaporated milk	1	tsp	Vanilla extract

In a 3-quart heavy saucepan, combine sugar, pudding mix, and milk. Cook over low heat, stirring constantly, until the temperature reaches 236°F or until a drop from a spoon into ice water forms a soft ball. Remove from heat and add butter. Beat until fudge cools and begins to thicken. Add nuts and continue to stir until fudge loses its gloss. Drop by spoonfuls onto wax paper. Allow fudge to harden at room temperature, and then cut into squares. Store in covered container.

CHOCOLATE RASPBERRY TRUFFLES

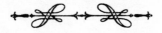

Ingredients:

2	Tbs	Raspberry liqueur	6	oz	Raspberry
4	Tbs	Whipping cream			chocolate chips
2	Tbs	Butter			

Coating:

6	oz	Bittersweet chocolate	2	Tbs	Butter

Heat liqueur in a heavy saucepan over high heat about 30 seconds, until liqueur is reduced by half.   Add cream and bring to a boil. Reduce heat and simmer 30 seconds.   Remove from heat and add butter and Semisweet chocolate chips.   Stir until mixture is smooth and melted.   Refrigerate 1 to 2 hours or until firm. Shape chilled chocolate mixture into 12 balls, about 1-1/2 inches in diameter.

Place balls on foil-lined plate; freeze for 1 hour.   Make coating: In top of double boiler, combine bittersweet chocolate and butter.   Place over water heated to 120°F.   Let stand 5 minutes; gently stir with wooden spoon until mixture is melted and smooth.   Remove pan and set aside. Add enough cold water to hot water to lower water temperature to about 90°F.   Place pan with chocolate over warm water and, stirring occasionally, let stand until chocolate is 86°F to 90°F.   Remove chocolate centers from freezer.   Dip, one at a time, into melted chocolate, turning to coat all sides.   Arrange on foil-lined plate.   Repeat until all 12 centers are coated.   Spoon leftover chocolate onto truffles for thicker coating. Refrigerate until serving time.

CHOCOLATE TAFFY

Ingredients:

2	Tbs	Butter	2/3	cup	Cocoa powder
1-1/2	cup	Light corn syrup	4	tsp	White vinegar
1/2	cup	Evaporated milk	1/4	tsp	Salt
2-1/2	cups	Sugar			

You will need one or two kitchen helpers to make this candy. Combine milk, corn syrup, and sugar in a large heavy saucepan. Bring to a boil over medium heat. Add cocoa powder, butter, salt, and vinegar and continue to boil with constant stirring until mixture reaches the firm-ball stage (or until candy thermometer reaches 248°F). Pour into a buttered pan and let cool until it can be handled without burning. Have two "taffy pullers" use buttered hands to work (fold over and pull -- using only finger tips -- again and again) the taffy until it is hard to pull. Pull into a twisted rope about 1/2" thick and cut into 1" sections. Let cool on waxed paper. Makes about 100 pieces.

CHOCOLATE WALNUT CARAMELS

Ingredients:

4	oz	Semisweet chocolate	1/2	cup	Milk
2	Tbs	Butter	1/2	cup	Sugar
1	cup	Molasses	2	tsp	Vanilla extract
1	cup	Walnut pieces			

Butter an 8-inch square pan. Set aside. Melt butter in heavy saucepan over medium heat and then add milk, sugar and molasses and, stirring constantly, bring to a boil. When mixture begins to boil, add chocolate and raise heat to medium–high. Stir occasionally to prevent mixture from sticking and burning. Continue cooking until mixture reaches the soft crack stage (280-290°F). Remove from heat and beat for three minutes, then stir in walnuts and vanilla, until thoroughly mixed. Turn into prepared pan. When cold, cut into one-inch squares and wrap in wax paper.

CHRISTMAS RIBBON CANDY

Ingredients:

3	cups	Sugar
1	cup	Light corn syrup
1/4	cup	Water
6-8	drops	Peppermint oil or cinnamon oil
1/4	tsp	Red paste food coloring
1/4	tsp	Green paste food coloring
2-3	pairs	White cotton work gloves

You will need one or two kitchen helpers to make this candy. Butter 3 shallow baking pans; set aside. Combine sugar, corn syrup, & water in buttered 4-quart saucepan. Cook over medium-high heat to boiling, stirring constantly with wooden spoon to dissolve sugar. Avoid splashing mixture on sides of pan. Cook over medium heat, stirring occasionally, for about 20 minutes or until mixture reaches

33

the soft crack stage (280°F on a candy thermometer). Remove from heat and stir in peppermint or cinnamon oil. Pour about one-half of the mixture into the first buttered pan. Pour half of the remaining candy into a 2-quart saucepan. Blend red coloring into this portion and pour into another buttered pan. Blend green coloring into the remaining portion in the four-quart saucepan. Pour in remaining buttered pan. Let candy cool slightly, 3-5 minutes for larger, uncolored portion, 1-2 minutes for smaller, red and green portions. As edges cool, lift and fold edges to center with metal spatula. (If candy sticks to spatula, let cool a few minutes longer before trying to work with it) When red and green candy can be rolled into balls with spatula, they are ready for shaping. With gloved hands, pull and twist red candy until light in color, about three minutes. Shape into a rope about 6-inches long. Place in one of the buttered pans and keep warm in a 200°F oven. Repeat with green portion. At the same time, have another person pull uncolored portion until white. Shape into 6" rope. Place white rope in center of 1 of the buttered baking sheets; place a colored rope on each side of white rope. Press all 3 ropes together to form a single flat log. Working quickly, have one person stretch one end of striped candy log lengthwise, until ribbon narrows to about 1" wide and is about 3/16 inch thick. Have second person immediately follow first person and turn ribbon onto 1 edge and fold accordion-style to make traditional ribbon shape. Break off in 6" lengths. If candy hardens too much, return to oven 3-5 min to soften. Yield: 2 pounds.

COBBLESTONE SQUARES

Ingredients:

12	oz	Butterscotch pieces	1	cup	Walnuts, chopped
1-1/2	cup	Miniature marshmallows	1	Tbs	Shortening

Grease an 8-inch square pan with wax paper. Combine butterscotch pieces and shortening in a large microwaveable bowl and microwave on high for one minute. Stir until melted. Microwave on high in additional 15 second intervals if necessary, stirring vigorously after each interval, to complete melting. Do not overcook. Stir in marshmallows and coarsely chopped walnuts. Spread mixture into prepared pan. Refrigerate several hours or until firm. Let stand at room temperature 5-10 minutes before cutting into squares.

COCOA FUDGE

Ingredients:

1/2	cup	Light corn syrup	1/4	cup	Butter
1/2	cup	Cocoa powder	2	cups	Sugar
1	tsp	Vanilla extract	1	cup	Milk
1	cup	Pecans, chopped			

In a medium saucepan, combine milk, sugar, cocoa, and corn syrup. Cook over high heat for 5 minutes, stirring constantly. Reduce heat; continue stirring until mixture forms a hard ball when dropped in a cup of cold water (264°F on a candy thermometer). Add butter and vanilla, but don't stir. Set aside to cool. When cool, beat until fudge begins to harden. Stir in pecans. Spread into a greased 9-inch pie pan. When cool, cut into squares. Store in covered container.

COCONUT BONBONS

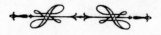

Ingredients:

1/2	cup	Butter	1/2	tsp	Vanilla extract
8	oz	Cream cheese	2	cups	Coconut
2	lbs	Confectioners' sugar			

Chocolate Coating:

12	oz	Semisweet chocolate chips	1/2	block	Paraffin

Combine butter, cream cheese, sugar and salt.   Add coconut. Refrigerate until cool and you can handle them.   Roll into small egg shapes. Refrigerate again. Coat with melted chocolate and paraffin. Chocolate Coating: In the top of a double boiler over simmering water, melt together paraffin and semisweet chocolate chips.   Stir until smooth.   Drop bonbons in chocolate.   Remove with fork and place on a buttered wax paper. When dry, place in paper candy cups.

COCONUT RUM BALLS

Ingredients:

2-1/2	cup	Crushed vanilla wafer cookies	3	tsp	Light corn syrup
			2	tsp	Cocoa
1	cup	Confectioners' sugar	1/2	cup	Rum
3-1/2	oz	Sweetened coconut	1/2	cup	Minced pecans

Mix together vanilla wafers, confectioners' sugar, nuts, coconut and cocoa. Add corn syrup, and rum. Mix well with hands and roll into 1-1/4 inch balls. Roll in confectioners' sugar.   Store in covered container for two to three days before serving for best flavor.

COOL LEMON FUDGE

Ingredients:

3	cups	Miniature marshmallows	1/4	cup	Butter
1/2	cup	Macadamia nuts, or pecans	12	oz	White chocolate chips
1/3	cup	Lemon juice	2-1/2	cup	Sugar
2	tsp	Lemon extract	5	oz	Evaporated milk

Line a 9-inch square pan with buttered aluminum foil and set aside. Place white chocolate chips, extracts and nuts into a microwaveable dish and set aside. Set butter aside to soften. Butter the sides and bottom of a 4-quart saucepan. In the saucepan, combine sugar and evaporated milk. Stirring constantly, cook mixture over medium heat until the sugars dissolve and the mixture begins to boil. Continue to cook for about six minutes, stirring the mixture occasionally to prevent scorching, until the temperature reaches 236°F or until a drop from a spoon into ice water forms a soft ball. Remove from heat and beat in marshmallows and butter until both have dissolved. Add lemon juice Return to burner bring to a boil again. Boil for five minutes over medium heat, stirring occasionally to avoid scorching. Mixture will turn light brown while cooking. Remove from heat and beat in white chocolate chips until melted. Allow the mixture to cool until about 110°F. Add lemon extract and then beat until fudge starts to thicken and loses its gloss. Quickly add nuts and pour into prepared pan. When fudge is cool, cut into squares.

COFFEE FUDGE

Ingredients:

3	cup	Sugar	1/4	cup	Butter
2	Tbs	Instant powdered coffee	1	tsp	Vanilla
1-1/4	cups	Light cream	1-1/2	cups	Chopped pecans
2	Tbs	Light corn syrup			

Combine sugar, coffee, cream and syrup in saucepan. Stirring constantly, cook over medium heat until sugar mixture comes to a boil and sugar dissolves. Contine cooking, stirring occasionally, to 238°F, or soft ball stage. Remove from heat; add butter and let cool, without stirring, until lukewarm. Add vanilla and beat until it begins to thicken, add nuts and continue to beat until fudge loses its gloss. Turn into buttered 8" square pan, or drop by teaspoonful onto buttered baking sheet.

CREAM CHEESE CHOCOLATE FUDGE

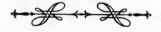

Ingredients:

4	cups	Confectioners' sugar	1	tsp	Vanilla extract
8	oz	Cream cheese	1	dash	Salt
4	oz	Unsweetened chocolate	1/2	cup	Chopped nuts

Butter an eight-inch square pan. Beat cream cheese until smooth, and then gradually add sifted confectioners' sugar until thoroughly combined. Chop chocolate into small pieces and place in a microwaveable bowl. Microwave on high for one minute, and then stir until chocolate is completely melted. Add vanilla and melted chocolate to mixture; blend thoroughly. Stir in nuts and spread into prepared pan and refrigerate overnight. Cut into squares.

CREAMY CAJUN PRALINES

Ingredients:

2	cups	Heavy cream	2	cups	Pecan halves
2	cups	Dark brown sugar	2	Tbs	Butter
1	Tbs	Vanilla			

Line a large cookie sheet with buttered wax paper. Set aside. Butter a large heavy saucepan. Pour in the cream, place over high heat and bring to a boil. Add the sugars and stir until dissolved and then add the pecans and vanilla. Continue cooking over medium heat stirring frequently, until the temperature reaches 236°F or until a drop from a spoon into ice water forms a soft ball. Remove from heat and quickly beat in the butter with a large wooden spoon until the candy loses its gloss and begins to cloud and become thick. Drop good-sized spoonfuls onto the buttered waxed paper, Allow to cool forty-five minutes to an hour and then remove from wax paper Store pralines in covered container with, with layers of waxed paper in between. Makes 2 to 3 dozen.

CREAMY SAVANNAH PRALINES

Ingredients:

1	lb	Light brown sugar	1	pinch	Salt
3/4	cup	Evaporated milk	2	cups	Pecan halves

Combine sugar, milk and salt together in heavy saucepan. Cook over low heat, stirring constantly until sugar is dissolved. Continue cooking and stirring over medium heat until the temperature reaches 236°F or until a drop from a spoon into ice water forms a soft ball. Cool slightly; beat until mixture begins to thicken. Add pecans and quickly drop candy by tablespoon on sheet of foil or well-buttered cookie sheet.

CRÈME DE MENTHE BALLS

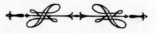

Ingredients:

1	cup	Vanilla wafer crumbs	2	tsp	White corn syrup
3/4	cup	Minced pecans	1/3	cup	White crème de
1	cup	Confectioners' sugar			menthe

Thoroughly mix all ingredients together and then form into 1-1/4 inch balls. Roll balls in additional confectioners' sugar and set on wax paper lined pan. Cover with additional wax paper and chill overnight. Age for a few days for best flavor.

CRISPY CRUNCHIES

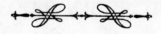

Ingredients:

18	oz	Peanut butter	3	cups	Crispy rice cereal
1	lb	Confectioners' sugar	1/2	cup	Butter

Chocolate coating:

12	oz	Semisweet chocolate chips	1/2	block	Paraffin

In a large mixing bowl, beat peanut butter, butter and powdered sugar together. Stir in crispy rice cereal. Blend with buttered hands until crumbly, and then squeeze dough into 1-1/4 inch balls. Melt chocolate chips and cake paraffin in double boiler. Dip balls in chocolate mixture and place on waxed paper to dry. Drizzle any excess chocolate over the completed candy.

CRISPY CRUNCHY FUDGE

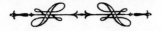

Ingredients:

1/4	cup	Butter	1/4	cup	Light corn syrup
1	cup	Semi-sweet	1	tsp	Vanilla extract
		chocolate chips	2	cups	Crispy rice cereal
1-1/2	cups	Confectioners' sugar			

Into a large saucepan over low heat, melt butter, chocolate chips, corn syrup and vanilla. Stir constantly until smooth. Remove from heat. Stir in sugar until well combined. Add cereal. Stir until evenly coated Press mixture into 8-inch square pan. Refrigerate until firm. Cut into squares.

CROCKPOT SUGARED WALNUTS

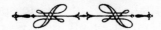

Ingredients:

1	lb	Walnuts, shelled	1/4	tsp	Ginger
1/2	cup	Butter, melted	1/4	tsp	Allspice
1/2	cup	Powdered sugar	1/8	tsp	Ground cloves
1-1/2	tsp	Cinnamon			

Combine walnuts and melted butter in a 3-1/2 quart slow cooker. Stir in powdered sugar until evenly coated. Cover and slow-cook on high for 15 minutes. Reduce the heat to low and slow cook about 2 hours, uncovered, stirring occasionally, until the nuts are coated with a crisp glaze. Transfer coated nuts to a serving bowl. In a small bowl, combine the spices and sift them over the nuts, stirring to coat evenly. Cool the nuts completely before serving.

DOUBLE DECKER FUDGE

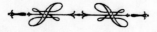

Ingredients:

Peanut butter fudge layer:

1	cup	Peanut butter chips
7	oz	Sweetened condensed milk (1/2 can)
2	Tbs	Butter, softened
1/2	tsp	Vanilla extract, divided

Chocolate fudge layer:

7	oz	Sweetened condensed milk (1/2 can)
1	cup	Semisweet chocolate chips
1/2	tsp	Vanilla extract, divided

Line 8-inch square pan with greased foil, letting foil extend on either side of pan to serve as handles. Place peanut butter chips, sweetened condensed milk and butter in microwave-safe bowl, microwave bowl at HIGH 1 - 2 minutes or until chips are melted and mixture is smooth when stirred; stir in 1/2-teaspoon vanilla extract. Immediately pour and spread evenly into prepared pan. Place chocolate chips and sweetened condensed milk in second microwave-safe bowl, microwave at HIGH 1-2 minute or until chips are melted and mixture is smooth when stirred; stir in 1/2-teaspoon vanilla extract. Immediately pour and spread evenly over peanut butter layer; cool. Cover and refrigerate until firm. Using the foil as handles, lift fudge from pan and place on cutting board. Peel off foil and cut fudge into 1-inch squares. Store in tightly covered container in refrigerator.

DOUBLE-DIPPED GOURMET APPLES

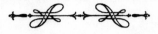

Ingredients:

2	cups	Semisweet chocolate Chips	5	med	Apples
1	Tbs	Solid Shortening	5	each	Wooden sticks
1	cup	Chopped pecans	48	each	Caramels

Wash and dry each apple. Insert a wooden stick into each apple. Line a large pan or tray with waxed paper. In medium microwave-safe bowl, microwave caramels on HIGH for 1-1/2 minutes or until caramels are softened. Stir until melted. If necessary after stirring to further melt caramels, microwave on high an additional 15 seconds. Stir until thoroughly melted. Do not overcook. Dip apples in caramels and set aside to harden. Next day, in medium microwave-safe bowl microwave chocolate chips and shortening on HIGH for 1 minute or until chips are softened   Stir until melted. If necessary after stirring to further melt chips, microwave on high an additional 15 seconds. Dip caramel apples into melted chocolate, leaving some caramel exposed. While removing the apple from the chocolate mixture, twirl to remove excess coating. Dip lower half of coated apple in chopped pecans. Allow to cool on prepared tray.

EASY FAUX FRENCH TRUFFLES

Ingredients:

8	oz	Unsweetened chocolate	14	oz	Sweetened condensed milk
4	oz	German sweet chocolate			
1	cup	Minced nuts			

Melt chocolates together in a heavy saucepan over very low heat, stirring constantly until smoothly blended. Add condensed milk and mix until smooth and well blended. Refrigerate for an hour and then shape into one-inch balls. Roll in Minced nuts until completely covered. Makes about 4-5 dozen.

EASY SUGAR COATED PEANUTS

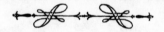

Ingredients:

16	oz	Cocktail peanuts	1/2	tsp	Nutmeg
3/4	cup	Sugar	1	large	Egg white
1	tsp	Salt	1	tsp	Water
2-1/2	tsp	Cinnamon			

Mix dry ingredients. Beat egg white until foamy and then add water, and continue to beat for one minute. Add nuts to egg and water mixture, then toss nuts in dry mixture until well coated. Spread nuts in single layer on cookie sheet. Bake at 325°F for 20 minutes. Separate while warm. Store in original peanut can.

ENGLISH TOFFEE

Ingredients:

1	cup	Sugar	3/4	cup	Light cream
3/4	cup	Light corn syrup	1/8	tsp	Salt

Combine sugar, cream, corn syrup and salt together in heavy saucepan. Cook over low heat, stirring constantly until sugar is dissolved. Continue cooking and stirring over medium heat until the temperature reaches 236°F or until a drop from a spoon into ice water forms a soft ball. Pour thin layer on greased slab. While warm, mark in squares. When thoroughly cooled, separate and wrap in wax paper when cold.

FOUR FLAVOR FUDGE

Ingredients:

2	cups	Milk chocolate chips	3/4	cup	Butter
7	oz	Marshmallow crème	1	tsp	Almond extract
14	oz	Sweetened condensed milk	2	cups	Peanut butter chips
			1	cup	Butterscotch chips
2	cups	Semisweet chocolate chips	3	Tbs	Milk
1-1/2	tsp	Vanilla extract	1	lb	Walnuts or pecans, coarsely chopped

Melt butter in a heavy stockpot over low heat; stir in sweetened condensed milk and regular milk. Add all chips and stir constantly until all chips have melted and mixture is smooth. Remove from heat; stir in marshmallow cream and flavorings. Stir in walnuts and spread evenly in a buttered 15 x 10-inch jellyroll pan. Chill and cut into squares. Store in the refrigerator. Yields 5 pounds.

FORGOTTEN KISSES

Ingredients:

1/2	cup	Chopped pecans	3	large	Egg whites
30	each	Chocolate kisses	1	pinch	Salt
1	cup	Sugar			

Preheat oven to 400°F. Beat the egg whites with the sugar, adding the sugar a little at a time until thoroughly incorporated; add salt and continue to beat until stiff peaks form and hold. Gently fold in nuts. Drop the batter by teaspoonfuls on greased cookie sheet, top with a chocolate kiss and then cover completely with more meringue. Place in pre-heated oven and turn the oven off. Leave in oven at least 6 hours or overnight. Do not open the oven. In the morning, carefully remove puffs from cookie sheet and store in airtight container.

FRUIT GUMMY GELS

Ingredients

2-1/2	cups	Boiling fruit juice	12 oz	Gelatin, any flavor

Stir boiling juice into gelatin in large bowl until completely dissolved, about three minutes. Pour into 13x9-inch pan. Chill overnight or until firm. Dip bottom of pan in warm water about 15 seconds. Cut into decorative shapes with cookie cutters all the way through gelatin or cut into 1-inch squares. Lift from pan.

GELATIN POPCORN BALLS

Ingredients:

1	cup	Light corn syrup	1-1/2	cups	Salted peanuts;
1/2	cup	Sugar			coarsely chop
3	oz	Gelatin, any flavor	9	cups	Popped popcorn

Bring syrup and sugar to a boil in saucepan over medium heat. Remove from heat, add gelatin and stir until dissolved. Add peanuts and pour over popcorn. Stir to coat popcorn. While still warm and sticky, quickly form into 1-1/2" popcorn balls. Makes about 4 dozen popcorn balls.

GOO GOO BARS

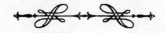

Ingredients:

14	oz	Sweetened	2	Tbs	Butter
		condensed milk	2	cups	Miniature
12	oz	Semisweet			marshmallows
		chocolate chips	2	cups	Chopped pecans

Combine butter, sweetened condensed milk, and chocolate chips in a large microwaveable bowl and microwave on HIGH for 2 minutes. Beat until smooth. When lukewarm, stir in nuts and marshmallows. Press into buttered 9x13 inch pan. Chill for 1 hour. Cut into squares.

GOURMET MARBLE SLAB CHOCOLATE FUDGE

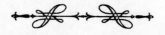

Ingredients:

4	cups	Confectioners' sugar	2	tsp	Vanilla extract
1/2	cup	Corn syrup	1/3	cup	Cocoa
1/2	tsp	Salt	1	cup	Chopped nuts
1-1/4	cup	Whipping cream			

Butter one 9x13x2 inch pan. Combine all ingredients (except pecans and flavorings) into a buttered 8-quart heavy stockpot. Stir constantly with a wooden spoon over low heat until butter melts and the sugar dissolves. Increase heat to medium and bring to a boil. Stir occasionally to prevent scorching and continue to boil about 6 minutes until the temperature reaches 236°F or until a drop from a spoon into ice water forms a soft ball. Remove saucepan from heat and add vanilla extract without stirring. Place pot in 3/4 inch of cool water place in the sink or a pan; allow fudge to cool to 110°F. Once fudge cools, beat vigorously until fudge loses its gloss and starts to thicken. Immediately add nuts before fudge totally hardens. Pour into prepared pan, score, and when cool cut into pieces and store in airtight container. This recipe freezes well.

GOURMET PEANUT BUTTER FUDGE

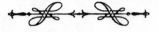

Ingredients:

4	cups	Confectioners' sugar	1/2	tsp	Salt
1	cup	Light corn syrup		tsp	Vanilla extract
1	cup	Chopped peanuts	1	cup	Peanut butter
1-1/2	cup	Whipping cream			

Butter one 9x13x2 inch pan. Combine all ingredients (except peanuts and flavorings) into a buttered 8-quart heavy stockpot. Stir constantly with a wooden spoon over low heat until butter melts and the sugar dissolves. Increase heat to medium and bring to a boil. Stir occasionally to prevent scorching and continue to boil about 6 minutes or until the temperature reaches 236°F or until a drop from a spoon into ice water forms a soft ball. Remove saucepan from heat and add vanilla extract without stirring. Place pot in 3/4 inch of cool water in the sink or a pan; allow fudge to cool to 110°F. Once fudge cools, beat vigorously until fudge loses its gloss and starts to thicken. Immediately add nuts before fudge totally hardens. Pour into prepared pan, score, and store when cool in airtight container. This recipe freezes well.

GRAND OPERA CREAMS

Ingredients:

Centers:

2	cups	Sugar	1/4	tsp	Salt
1-1/2	tsp	Vanilla extract	1	cup	Light cream
2	Tbs	Light corn syrup	2	Tbs	Butter

Chocolate Coating:

1/2	block	Paraffin	4	oz	Semisweet
2	Tbs	Shortening			chocolate chips

Combine sugar, salt, cream, butter and corn syrup in a heavy 2-1/2-quart saucepan. Bring to a boil, stirring constantly. Cook at a gentle boil, stirring frequently, until the mixture reaches 236°F or until a drop from a spoon into ice water forms a soft ball. Remove from heat and cool, without stirring, until mixture is 110°F. Add vanilla and beat vigorously until candy is thick and loses its gloss. Quickly drop by spoonfuls into mounds on waxed paper. If the candy gets too stiff and dry before this is completed, knead each dropped candy between fingers or roll between the palms of the hands. Let candy stand until firm to the touch. Chocolate Coating: In top of double boiler, mix shortening, paraffin and chocolate over boiling water. Spoon a small amount of chocolate glaze over each cream. Let stand until set. Wrap in wax paper and store in refrigerator. Makes about 24 candies.

HAYSTACKS

Ingredients:

2	cups	Brown sugar	1	Tbs	Butter
1	cups	Non-dairy liquid	1	tsp	Vanilla extract
		coffee cream	1	cup	Coconut

In a buttered heavy saucepan, combine all ingredients except coconut and cook over medium heat without stirring until the temperature reaches 236°F or until a drop from a spoon into ice water forms a soft ball. Remove from heat and allow to cool for 30 minutes. Beat cooled mixture until it begins to thicken and then stir in coconut. Drop by spoonfuls onto waxed paper in the shape of haystacks. Makes about 60 pieces.

HAWAIIAN PINEAPPLE PECAN FUDGE

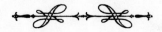

Ingredients:

4	cups	Sugar	2	Tbs	Butter
1	cup	Cream	1	cup	Pecans
1	cup	Pineapple chunks			

Butter a 9x13x2-inch pan and the sides of a heavy 4-quart saucepan. Combine sugar and cream in saucepan and cook over medium heat, stirring continually until sugar melts. Continue to cook until mixture comes to a boil. Boil for six minutes, or until the temperature reaches 236°F or until a drop from a spoon into ice water forms a soft ball. Remove from heat and add butter; beat for 5 minutes, until fudge begins to thicken and lose its gloss. Stir in pineapple and pecans. Pour into prepared pan. Allow to cool completely before cutting into 36 – 48 pieces.

HIGH SOCIETY TRUFFLES

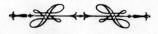

Ingredients:

4	cup	Confectioners' sugar	8	oz	Cream cheese, softened
1	tsp	Vanilla extract, rum cointreau or Kahlua	5	oz	Unsweetened chocolate

For rolling, choose one:

1/2	cup	Confectioners' sugar	1/2	cup	Cocoa
1/2	cup	Toasted almonds	1/2	cup	Toasted coconut

Melt chocolate in a saucepan over low heat, or microwave in a microwaveable bowl on high for one minute and stir until melted. Microwave on high in additional 15 second intervals if necessary, stirring vigorously after each interval, to complete melting. Do not overcook. Set aside. Gradually blend confectioners' sugar into softened cream cheese, mixing well after each addition. Stir in melted chocolate and vanilla extract; mix well. Chill for several hours. Shape into 1-1/4 inch balls; roll in almonds, cocoa or the topping of your choice. Chill. Store in a covered container in refrigerator until ready to serve.

HONEY TAFFY

Ingredients:

1	cup	Sugar	1	pinch	Cream of tartar
1/2	cup	Light corn syrup	2	Tbs	Butter
1/2	cup	Honey	1	tsp	Vinegar

You will need one or two kitchen helpers to make this candy. Put the sugar, syrup and honey in a heavy 4-quart saucepan. On medium heat, cook until the sugar completely melts, then add cream of tartar and boil, stirring continuously for about 20 minutes. Add the vinegar and butter and let it return to boil, then remove from heat and pour into a buttered pan. Have two "taffy pullers" use buttered hands to work (fold over and pull -- using only finger tips -- again and again) the taffy until it is hard to pull. Pull into a twisted rope about 1/2" thick and cut into 1" sections. Let cool on waxed paper. Store in an airtight container between layers of waxed paper. Makes about 100 pieces.

KAHLÚA COCOA BALLS

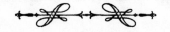

Ingredients:

1/2	cup	Kahlua liqueur	1/2	cup	Cocoa powder
1/4	cup	Light corn syrup	2-1/2	cup	Finely crushed
1/3	cup	Maraschino cherries			vanilla wafers
1/3	cup	Golden raisins	1	cup	Minced pecans
1	cup	Confectioners' sugar	1/2	tsp	Almond extract

Coating:

1/4	cup	Confectioners' sugar	2	Tbs	Cocoa

Combine Kahlua with corn syrup and chopped fruits. Blend sugar, cocoa, crumbs, almond extract and pecans. Thoroughly combine the two mixtures and shape into small balls. Combine confectioners' sugar and cocoa to make a dry coating. Roll balls in coating and store in an airtight container. Makes 48.

KITCHEN CANDY BARS

Ingredients:

1	lb	Confectioners' sugar	1/2	tsp	Vanilla extract
2/3	cup	Sweetened	1/2	tsp	Almond extract
		condensed milk	1	lb	Chopped nuts

Coating:

12	oz	Semisweet chocolate chips
12	oz	Butterscotch chips

Grease a 13x9x2-inch pan. Set aside. Combine confectioners' sugar, sweetened condensed milk, vanilla and almond extract in large bowl. Mix thoroughly, using hands to knead. Roll between two sheets of wax paper to form a 13x9 rectangle. Chill in refrigerator. Meanwhile, melt chocolate and butterscotch pieces in top of double boiler over hot water. Stir in nuts. Spread one half of chocolate mixture in buttered 13x9x2 baking pan. Carefully place fondant layer on top. Spread remaining chocolate-nut mixture on top. Refrigerate until firm. Remove from refrigerator ten minutes before cutting. Cut into bars. Store in covered container in refrigerator. Makes 48 pieces.

LEMON DROPS

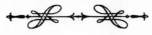

Ingredients:

2	drops	Yellow food coloring	1-1/2	tsp	Lemon extract *
1	cups	Light corn syrup	2	cups	Sugar
1/2	cups	Water			

Oil two cookie sheets or 65 fancy candy molds with vegetable oil. Combine sugar, corn syrup and water in a 4-quart heavy saucepan over high heat.   Bring quickly to a boil, while constantly stirring. With a pastry brush dipped in warm water, wipe sugar crystals from side of pan as mixture cooks.   Reduce heat to medium and cook, without stirring, to 300°F on a candy thermometer or until a little syrup dropped from a spoon will form brittle threads in cold water. Remove saucepan from heat and stir in oil of lemon and yellow food coloring. Continue to stir until mixture stops bubbling.   Pour syrup by spoonfuls into oiled molds or drop by teaspoonfuls on oiled cookie sheets. If misture becomes too hard to finish, place over very low

heat for a few minutes just until mixture thins, but not long enough for syrup to darken. Cool candies in molds at least one hour.   To remove candies: insert the tip of a small knife around edge of drops and lift up to loosen.   Store in layers, separated by foil or wax paper in a covered container.

*Note: You may use 1/2 tsp oil of lemon or orange in lieu of extracts.
For orange drops, increase yellow food coloring to 1/4 tsp and add 2 drops red food coloring and substitute 1/1/2 tsp orange extract for lemon.*

LOUISIANA CREAM FUDGE

Ingredients:

3	cups	Sugar	1/4	cup	Butter
2	cups	Whipping cream	1/2	cup	Flour
1	cup	Cornstarch	2	cups	Whole pecans

Butter a 9x13x2-inch pan and the sides of a heavy 4-quart saucepan. Put sugar, whipping cream and cornstarch in a saucepan over medium heat and cook until the temperature reaches 236°F or until a drop from a spoon into ice water forms a soft ball. Remove from heat and add butter; beat for 5 minutes. Blend in flour and beat until creamy and thick. Add whole pecans. When thick, pour into buttered pan. Allow to cool completely before cutting into 36 – 48 pieces.

MACKINAC ISLAND FUDGE

Ingredients:

4	cup	Confectioners' sugar	1/4	tsp	Salt
1	cup	Milk	2	tsp	Vanilla extract
1	cup	Butter	1/2	cup	Cocoa
1	cup	Brown sugar	1	cup	Walnuts
1	cup	Sugar			

Butter a 9x13x2 inch pan. Butter the sides of a 4-quart saucepan. Mix milk, butter, brown sugar, Sugar and salt in heavy saucepan. While stirring constantly, cook at medium heat until boiling. Boil for exactly 6 minutes, stirring constantly and then remove from heat. Immediately add cocoa, vanilla extract and confectioners' sugar. Beat with mixer until smooth and thick. Add nuts, if desired. Pour into a buttered pan and refrigerate for one hour. Cut into pieces

MAPLE FLUFFS

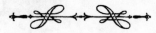

Ingredients:

1	cup	Maple syrup	1	cup	Miniature
1/2	cup	Brown sugar			marshmallows
1/2	cup	Water	1	large	Egg white
1/2	tsp	Cream of tartar	24	each	Walnut halves

In a heavy saucepan over medium-high heat, combine the maple syrup, brown sugar, water and cream of tartar, stirring until the sugar is completely dissolved and the mixture begins to boil. Cover the pan of boiling syrup and cook for 2 or 3 minutes to allow the steam to wash down the crystals from the sides of the pan. Remove the lid and cook without stirring over medium heat until the mixture reaches the hard ball stage, or 264°F on a candy thermometer. Remove from heat and stir in marshmallows until melted. Pour mixture over stiffly beaten white of egg. Beat up until light, and when it begins to harden, drop from teaspoon on oiled or greased paper. Place a half walnut in center of each piece. Set aside to cool.

MAPLE NUT FUDGE

Ingredients:

1	lb	Soft maple sugar	3/4	cup	Cream
1/4	cup	Boiling water	2/3	cup	English walnuts

Coarsely chop walnuts and set aside. Break sugar into small pieces; put into a saucepan with cream and water over medium heat. Bring to a boil and boil until the temperature reaches 236°F or until a drop from a spoon into ice water forms a soft ball. Remove from heat; beat until creamy. Add walnuts to mixture and pour into a buttered tin. Cool slightly, and cut into squares.

MAPLE NUT TRUFFLES

Ingredients:

1/2	cup	Butter, softened	8	oz.	Cream cheese
6	cups	Confectioners' sugar	1/2	cup	Maple syrup

Chocolate Coating:

16	oz	Semisweet chocolate chips	2	blocks	Paraffin
			1/2	cup	Shortening

Topping:

1	cup	Chopped nuts

In a mixing bowl, beat cream cheese, butter, confectioners' sugar and maple syrup until smooth. Cover and refrigerate for 1 hour. Shape into 1-inch balls. Chocolate Coating: In top of double boiler, mix shortening, paraffin and chocolate over boiling water. Using toothpicks, dip balls into chocolate; roll in nuts. Place on wax paper-lined baking sheets. Refrigerate. Yields about 8 dozen.

MARSHMALLOWS

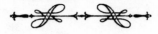

Ingredients:

1	Tbs	Light corn syrup	1-1/2	cups	Water
1	oz	Powdered gelatin	2	large	Egg whites
1	lb	Sugar	2	tsp	Vanilla extract

Dusting Mixture:

1	cup	Confectioners' sugar	2	Tbs	Cornstarch

Lightly grease a 13x9x2 inch pan and dust with confectioners' sugar and cornstarch. Beat egg whites until stiff peaks form. Set aside. In a double boiler, soak gelatin in 1/2 cup of water and vanilla for 5-10 minutes and then dissolve gelatin over simmering water. In a separate large heavy saucepan over medium heat, combine sugar, corn syrup and one cup of water. Stir constantly until the sugar is dissolved, then bring syrup to a boil without stirring. Increase heat and boil until the syrup reaches 260°F (hard ball stage). Add dissolved gelatin to corn syrup mixture and continue to cook for one

minute. While continually whisking, pour corn syrup mixture in a steady stream into the bowl containing stiffly beaten egg whites. Continue whisking until mixture becomes a thick white opaque mass that holds its shape. Pour mixture into prepared pan. Allow the mixture to set at room temperature for several hours. Dust a large sheet of wax paper with confectioners' sugar and turn marshmallow out onto it. Cut into squares and dust with confectioners' sugar and leave out to dry for at least an hour.

MARSHMALLOW CREAM

Ingredients:

1	cup	Sugar	1/2	cup	Water
1	Tbs	Unflavored gelatin	1-1/2	tsp	Cornstarch
1/2	cup	Light corn syrup	1	pinch	Cream of tartar
1/2	cup	Half-and-half	2	large	Egg whites

Combine the gelatin, cornstarch, and half-and-half in a small saucepan and let stand for 15 minutes. Heat the mixture over low head, stirring until the gelatin is dissolved. Do not boil. Keep warm. In a large bowl whip the egg whites with the cream of tartar and salt until stiff peaks form. In a separate 3-quart saucepan add the sugar, corn syrup, and water then bring to a boil over medium heat washing down any sugar crystals forming on the sides of the pan with a pastry brush and cool water. Continue to boil and mix by gentle swirling until the candy thermometer reaches 240°F. Pour the sugar syrup in a stream into the egg whites while beating. Now pour the gelatin mixture in a stream into the egg white/sugar while beating. Continue to beat until cool. Add vanilla, mix, and chill for at least 2 hours. Beat 1-2 minutes before serving.

MARSHMALLOW CRÈME DIVINITY

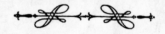

Ingredients:

7	oz	Marshmallow crème	1/2	cup	Water
1	cup	Chopped pecans or	1/8	tsp	Salt
		chopped maraschinos	1	tsp	Vanilla extract
2	cups	Sugar			

Boil sugar, water and salt in saucepan until mixture forms a hard ball in cold water (or 252°F on candy thermometer). Place marshmallow crème in large bowl; stir in hot syrup very slowly. Continue stirring until slightly stiff. Add vanilla extract and nuts (or cherries). Drop by spoonful onto wax paper.

MARTHA WASHINGTON CHOCOLATES

Ingredients:

Centers:

| 2 | lbs | Confectioners' sugar | 1/2 | cup | Butter |
| 14 | oz | Sweetened condensed milk | 1 | lb | Pecans, chopped |

Chocolate Coating:

| 8 | oz | Semisweet chocolate chips | 1 | block | Paraffin |
| | | | 1/4 | cup | Shortening |

Mix sugar, milk, 1/2-cup butter and pecans well. Roll in balls approximately 1" in diameter. Set aside. In top of double boiler, mix shortening, paraffin and chocolate over boiling water. Using toothpicks, dip balls into chocolate, set on waxed paper until cool.

Alternate Microwave Chocolate Coating Method: In a microwaveable container, combine chocolate chips, paraffin and shortening. Microwave on high for one and a half minutes. Stir until melted chips and shortening are completely blended. Microwave on high in additional 15 second intervals if necessary, stirring vigorously after each interval, to complete melting. Do not overcook.

MARZIPAN

Ingredients:

| 3/4 | cup | Confectioners' sugar | 1/2 | tsp | Almond extract |
| 8 | oz. | Almond paste | Food | coloring | as needed |

Beat all ingredients together *except food colors* on low speed until mixture forms a smooth paste. Tightly cover and refrigerate one hour. Divide dough into equal parts, depending upon how many different colors you would like, and the drop of food coloring into each and knead unto color is evenly blended. Shape dough in fruit shapes Store tightly covered in refrigerator or at room temperature.

61

MASHED POTATO CANDY

Ingredients:
| 3 | lbs | Confectioners' sugar | 1/2 | cup | Mashed potatoes |
| 2 | cups | Peanut butter | 1/4 | tsp | Salt |

Mix mashed potatoes, salt and powdered sugar together until you have stiff dough.   On wax paper, roll dough into a rectangle about 1/4 inch thick.   Spread peanut butter over dough.   Roll dough up using the wax paper as you would a jellyroll.   Cut into pinwheel candies.

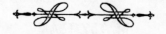

MELT AWAY LEMON PUFFS

Ingredients:
| 3 | large | Egg whites | 6 | Tbs | Sugar |
| 1/4 | tsp | Cream of tartar | 1 | Tbs | Lemon zest |

Preheat oven to 250°F.   Beat egg whites until foamy.   Add cream of tartar, and beat until soft peaks form.   Beat in sugar, one tablespoon at a time; continue beating until stiff and glossy peaks form.   Gently fold in lemon zest.   Drop mixture by heaping tablespoons onto 2 greased baking sheets.   Bake at 250°F oven 1 hour.   Turn off oven; do not open oven door.   Leave in oven undisturbed for 1 hour.   Then transfer to wire racks to cool completely.

MICROWAVE FUDGE

Ingredients:

3	cups	Semisweet chocolate chips	1/4	cup	Butter
14	oz	Sweetened condensed milk	1-1/2	tsp	Vanilla
1	cup	Chopped walnuts			

Combine chocolate chips and condensed milk in a microwaveable bowl. Microwave on medium until the chocolate chips are melted, 3 to 5 minutes. Stir twice during cooking to facilitate melting. Stir in nuts and vanilla. Pour fudge into greased, 8 X 8 baking pan and chill to set. Cut into on inch squares.

MICROWAVE HEAVENLY HASH FUDGE

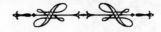

Ingredients:

1	cup	Miniature marshmallows	3	Tbs	Cocoa
1	lb	Confectioners' sugar	1	tsp	Vanilla
1/2	cup	Butter	1/2	cup	Chopped nuts
1/4	cup	Milk			

Slice butter and put into a microwaveable bowl with milk and cocoa. Microwave on HIGH for 2 minutes. Stir in sugar. Beat until smooth. Add vanilla and nuts. Microwave on HIGH for 30 seconds. Beat. Add marshmallows and pour into buttered 8-inch square pan. Cool and cut into squares.

MILK CHOCOLATE PRALINES

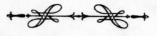

Ingredients:

12	oz	Milk chocolate chips	3/4	cup	Water
1	cup	Light brown sugar	2	cups	Sugar
1	cup	Pecans, chopped	1	tsp	Vinegar
1/4	cup	Light corn syrup	1/2	tsp	Salt

Pecan halves for decoration (optional)

In a large saucepan, over high heat combine Sugar, brown sugar, water, corn syrup, vinegar and salt. Bring to full boil, stirring constantly. Boil for 3 minutes without stirring. Remove from heat and cool at least five minutes. Add milk chocolate chips, stir quickly with wire whisk or wooden spoon until melted. Stir in pecans. Quickly drop by level measuring tablespoons onto cookie sheets lined with buttered foil. Garnish with pecan halves if desired. Refrigerate until set. Peel candies off foil when set. Store in refrigerator.

MINT & CHOCOLATE FUDGE

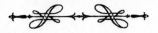

Ingredients:

Fudge Base:

4	cup	Confectioners' sugar	1/2	cup	Butter
1	tsp	Vanilla extract	3/4	cup	Cocoa
1/2	cup	Evaporated milk			

Pastel Mint Topping:

1-1/2	cup	Confectioners' sugar	1	Tbs	Water
2	drops	Green food coloring	1/4	tsp	Mint extract
3	Tbs	Butter			

Line 8-inch square pan with wax paper. Place butter in medium-size microwave-safe bowl, microwave at HIGH 1 to 1-1/2 minutes or until melted. Add cocoa; stir until smooth. Stir in confectioners' sugar and vanilla extract. Blend well until crumbly. Stir in evaporated milk. Microwave at HIGH 1 to 2 minutes or until mixture is hot. Beat until smooth and then immediately pour into prepared pan. Cover; chill until firm. Pastel Mint Topping: In small mixer bowl, beat butter, water and mint extract until blended. Gradually add confectioners' sugar and food color. Beat until smooth. Spread topping  evenly over fudge and then refrigerate until firm. Cut into 1-inch squares, cover and store in refrigerator.

MISSISSIPPI RIVERBOAT GAMBLERS

Ingredients:

50	each	Caramels	2	tsp	Butter
2	tsp	Water	3	cups	Halved pecans

Coating:

10	oz	Milk chocolate chips	1/2	block	Paraffin

Melt caramels, water and butter in microwave safe bowl on high for one minute. Stir until fully melted, Microwave in additional 15-second intervals if necessary, but be careful not to overcook. Stir in pecans until coated and then drop spoonfuls onto greased aluminum foil-covered cookie sheet. Cool. Melt chocolate chips and paraffin together in microwave safe bowl on high for one minute. Stir until fully melted. Microwave at additional 15-second intervals if necessary, but be careful not to overcook. Use ice pick or skewer to remove caramel-pecan drops from foil and dip in warmed chocolate mixture. Return dipped candy to foil to cool. Yields 3 to 4 dozen.

MILLIONAIRE KISSES

Ingredients:

14	oz	Caramels, unwrapped	2	Tbs	Butter
1	lb	Vanilla candy coating	2	Tbs	Water
1	cup	Semisweet chocolate chips	3	cups	Pecan halves

Cook caramels, butter and water in a heavy saucepan over low heat, stirring constantly until smooth. Stir in pecan halves. Cool in pan 5 minutes. Drop by spoonfuls onto lightly greased wax paper. Chill 1 hour, or freeze 20 minutes until firm. Melt chocolate chips and candy coating in a heavy saucepan over low heat, stirring until smooth. Using a fork, dip caramel candies into chocolate mixture, allowing excess to drip; place on lightly greased wax paper. Let stand until firm. Makes 4 dozen.

MOCHA ALMOND TRUFFLES

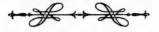

Ingredients:

1/2	cup	Whipping cream	1	cup	Semisweet
1/2	cup	Chopped almonds			chocolate chips
2	Tbs	Butter	1-1/2	tsp	Vanilla extract
1	Tbs	Instant coffee	2	Tbs	Sugar

In small saucepan combine whipping cream, sugar, butter and instant coffee; cook over low heat, stirring constantly, just until mixture boils. Remove from heat; immediately add chocolate chips. Stir until chips are melted and mixture is smooth when stirred. Add vanilla extract. Pour into small bowl; chill, stirring occasionally, until mixture begins to set. Cover and refrigerate overnight to allow mixture to ripen and harden. Work with one third of the mixture at a time, keeping the remainder refrigerated. Form mounded teaspoons of mixture into balls, quickly roll in nuts or grated chocolate. Tightly cover and store in refrigerator. Serve cold. Makes about 2-3 dozen truffles.

MOCK CHOCOLATE DIPPED STRAWBERRIES

Ingredients:

6	oz	Strawberry gelatin	3/4	cup	Sweetened
1	cup	Ground sweetened			condensed milk
		coconut	1/2	tsp.	Almond extract
1	cup	Ground pecans			

Coating:

12	oz	Semisweet chocolate chips	1	block	Paraffin

Grind pecans and coconut, or use a food processor to finely chop them. In a large bowl, combine gelatin, pecans, coconut, condensed milk and almond extract. Shape into balls, then set on wax paper. Place a toothpick in each ball and chill in the refrigerator overnight. The next day, melt paraffin and chocolate chips in a double boiler whisking until thoroughly blended. Dip mock strawberries into chocolate mixture. Set them on wax paper until dry. Makes about two-dozen mock chocolate dipped strawberries.

MOCK TURKISH DELIGHT

Ingredients:

2	cups	Sugar	1	Tbs	Orange extract
2	Tbs	Cornstarch	2	drops	Orange food coloring
1	cup	Water	1/2	cup	Toasted almonds
1/2	tsp	Cream of tartar			or pistachios

Confectioners' sugar for dusting

Grease and butter an 8-inch square pan. Set aside. In a heavy saucepan, stir together sugar, cornstarch and water until dissolved. Add cream of tartar and over medium heat bring to a boil. When temperature reaches 220°F, cover pot and cook undisturbed for five minutes. Remove from heat and add orange extract, food coloring and nuts. Pour mixture into prepared pan. Refrigerate overnight. Next day, cut into squares and roll each piece in sifted powdered sugar. Store in plastic bag or covered container.

MOLASSES TAFFY

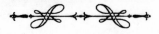

Ingredients:

1/2	cup	Molasses	1/4	tsp	Cream of tartar
1-1/2	cup	Sugar	1/4	cup	Butter, softened
1/2	cup	Water	1/8	tsp	Baking soda
1-1/2	Tbs	Cider vinegar	1/2	tsp	Vanilla extract

Grease a cookie sheet, 9 x 13 pan or marble slab. Blend the molasses, sugar, water and cider vinegar in a heavy 3-quart saucepan. Bring to a boil over medium-low heat. Add cream of tartar. Cover and let boil 3 minutes. Uncover and brush down sugar crystals from sides of pan using pastry brush dipped into cool water. Continue to boil with minimal stirring until the temperature reaches 256°F (hard ball stage). Remove from heat and add butter, baking soda, and vanilla. Pour out onto prepared sheet or slab. Use a spatula to fold the edges of the cooling taffy toward the center. When cool enough to handle butter your fingertips and find a friend, child, or spouse (have them butter their hands, too). Pull the taffy about 12 inches, twist, and fold back on itself. Repeat this process until the taffy becomes difficult to pull. Pull and roll into a long rope and cut with buttered scissors into small bite-sized segments. Place on waxed paper to harden. Store in an airtight container between layers of waxed paper. Makes about 1 pound.

OATMEAL PEANUT BUTTER CAFETERIA FUDGE

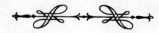

Ingredients:

2	cups	Sugar	1	tsp	Vanilla extract
1/2	cup	Milk	1/2	cup	Peanut butter
1/2	cup	Butter	2	cups	Quick oats
1/4	cup	Cocoa			

Line an 8x8 inch pan with greased wax paper. In a 4-quart heavy bottom saucepan, combine sugar, milk, butter and cocoa over medium heat. Stirring constantly, bring to a boil, and continue to cook for 6 minutes. Remove from heat; beat in vanilla extract and peanut butter until thoroughly mixed. Stir in oats and mix thoroughly. Pour into prepared pan and let cool. Cut into squares.

OLD FASHIONED BUTTERSCOTCH FUDGE

Ingredients:

1/2	cup	Butter	2	cup	Brown sugar
1-1/2	cup	Sour cream	2	tsp	Vanilla extract
2	cup	Sugar	1/2	tsp	Salt
1/4	cup	White corn syrup	1	cup	Chopped nuts

Butter a 9x13x2 inch pan. Set aside. Butter the sides and bottom of a 4-quart saucepan. In the saucepan, combine brown sugar, butter, Sugar, sour cream, and salt over low heat and stir until the sugar is melted. Increase to medium heat and bring to a boil, stirring occasionally to prevent scorching. Boil over medium heat until the temperature reaches 236ºF or until a drop from a spoon into ice water forms a soft ball. Set the pan in the sink in about an inch of cold water, add vanilla extract and cool until lukewarm (110ºF). Remove from sink and beat until fudge begins to thicken and lose its gloss. Quickly stir in nuts and pour into prepared pan. Allow to firm but not harden before cutting into squares.

OPERA FUDGE

Ingredients:

2	cup	Sugar	2	Tbs	Butter
1	cup	Heavy cream	1/2	tsp	Vanilla extract
1/8	tsp	Salt	Few grains Salt		

Line an 8x8 inch pan with greased wax paper. Put sugar, cream and few grains of salt into a 4-quart saucepan. While stirring continuously, cook over moderate heat. When at the boiling point, add 1/8-teaspoon salt. Continue cooking until candy thermometer reaches 236°F or until a drop from a spoon into ice water forms a soft ball. Remove from heat and add butter and vanilla. Allow to melt, then beat until fudge thickens and loses its gloss. Cover with a damp cloth and let stand 1/2 hour. Press into pan and then, when firm cut into 32 squares.

OPERA NUT CREAMS

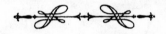

Ingredients:

2	cups	Sugar	1	tsp.	Vanilla
3/4	cup	Heavy cream	3/4	cup	Chopped walnuts
1/2	cup	Milk	6	oz	Semi-sweet
1	Tbs	Light corn syrup			chocolate chips
1/8	tsp	Salt	Whole walnuts for garnish		

Stir together sugar, syrup, cream, milk, and salt in a 4-quart saucepan until well mixed. Bring to a boil on medium heat. Place thermometer in mixture and cook to 236°F (soft ball stage). Remove from heat and allow to cool to 110°F without stirring. Add vanilla and beat until mixture loses its gloss. Add nuts. Spoon into buttered 8-inch square pan. Cool to firm. Microwave chocolate on HIGH for 1-2 minutes. Stir until melted and then spread over top. Score and garnish with whole walnuts. Chill until firm and then cut into squares. Makes about 2 pounds.

ORANGE CHOCOLATE MELT-AWAYS

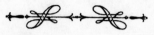

Ingredients:

3	cups	Finely crushed vanilla wafers	1	cup	Minced pecans
2	Tbs	Orange juice concentrate	2	Tbs	Light corn syrup
1	cup	Confectioners' sugar	1	Tbs	Grand Marnier

Topping:

1-1/2	cups	Semisweet chocolate chips
1-1/2	Tbs	Solid shortening

Place vanilla wafer crumbs in a bowl. Add pecans and sugar. Mix well, mashing out lumps of sugar with the back of the spoon. Work in the orange concentrate and corn syrup, then the liqueur. Blend thoroughly. Butter your hands lightly and shape dough into 1-1/4 inch balls, using a mounded soupspoon or tablespoon as measure. Flatten slightly so they do not roll, and place the candies on jellyroll

pans or trays lined with wax paper. Freeze overnight. Next morning, in a heavy saucepan, melt shortening and chocolate chips over low heat. Working with one dozen balls at a time, place each ball on a fork and dip into chocolate mixture. Transfer patties to a jellyroll pan lined with wax paper. Chill until chocolate hardens. Store in an airtight container in the refrigerator. Yields about 2-3 dozen melt-away balls.

ORANGE ICE

Ingredients:

1-3/4	oz	Powdered fruit pectin	1	cup	Sugar
3	drops	Orange food coloring	1	cup	Light corn syrup
3/4	cup	Water	2	tsp	Orange extract
1/2	tsp	Baking soda			

Coating:

6	Tbs	Confectioners' sugar	2	Tbs	Cornstarch

Combine fruit pectin, water and baking soda in a medium-size saucepan. Combine sugar and corn syrup in large heavy saucepan. Place both saucepans over high heat. Cook, stirring alternately, until the foam disappears from the fruit pectin mixture and the sugar mixture begins to boil rapidly (about 5 minutes). Gradually add fruit pectin mixture in a thin steady stream to boiling sugar mixture until all pectin is added. Boil mixture, stirring constantly, 1 minute longer. Remove saucepan from heat. Stir in orange extract and orange food coloring. Immediately pour mixture into an 8x8x2" pan lined with

wax paper. Allow to stand at room temperature at least 4 hours, or until candy is cool and firm. Cut gumdrop mixture into fancy shapes with small cutters or cut into cubes with a knife dipped in warm water. Put a few pieces at a time in a plastic bag containing powdered sugar and cornstarch mixed together; shake to coat. Makes 3-4 dozen.

ORANGE SNOWBALLS

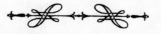

Ingredients:

3	cups	Finely crushed vanilla wafers	1	cup	Nuts, chopped
1/3	cup	Butter, melted	1/4	cup	Frozen orange juice concentrate
1	cup	Confectioners' sugar	1	tsp	Orange extract

Coating:

1-1/2 cups   White chocolate chips   1-1/2 Tbs   Solid shortening

Decoration:

1   cup   Sweetened flake coconut

Combine vanilla wafer crumbs, melted butter, confectioners' sugar, nuts, orange juice and orange extract; shape into small balls. Freeze overnight. Next morning, in microwaveable bowl, melt shortening and white chocolate chips on high for 1-1/2 to 2 minutes. Stir until blended. Working with one dozen balls at a time, place each ball on a fork and dip into the white chocolate mixture then roll in coconut. Place on wax paper to dry and then store for 2-3 days before serving for best flavor. Makes 3-4 dozen candies.

PEACHES & CREAM FUDGE

Ingredients:

1	Tbs	Peach-flavored schnapps	3/4	tsp	Baking soda
3	oz	Box peach gelatin	8	oz	Peach yogurt
1	cup	Sour cream	2	Tbs	Butter
3	cups	Confectioners' sugar			

Butter a 9-inch square-baking dish. Butter the sides of a heavy 4-quart saucepan. Combine sugar, sour cream, baking soda, gelatin and yogurt in saucepan. Cook over medium heat, stirring constantly, until sugar and gelatin dissolves and mixture comes to a boil. Cook until the temperature reaches 236°F or until a drop from a spoon into ice water forms a soft ball, stirring occasionally to prevent scorching. Immediately remove from heat, add butter (do not stir) and cool to lukewarm (110°F). Add schnapps and beat vigorously until mixture thickens and loses its gloss. Quickly spread into prepared pan. Score while warm, and cut into squares when firm. Store in a covered container.

PEANUT BUTTER BONBONS

Ingredients:
Centers

18	oz	Peanut butter	2	cups	Butter, softened
4	lbs	Confectioners' sugar	8	oz	Cream cheese

Chocolate Coating:

8	oz	Semisweet chocolate chips	1/2	block	Paraffin

Cream together the peanut butter, cream cheese and butter. Slowly add sugar; mix well. Roll into 1 inch balls. Chill until firm. Chocolate coating: Melt together in the top of a double boiler 1/2 block paraffin and 8 oz semisweet chocolate. Stir until smooth. Drop bonbons in chocolate remove with spoon and place on buttered wax paper. When dry, place in paper candy cups.

Alternate Microwave Method for Chocolate Coating: In a microwaveable container, combine chocolate chips and paraffin. Microwave on high for one and a half minutes. Stir until melted chips and shortening are completely blended. Microwave on high in additional 15 second intervals if necessary, stirring vigorously after each interval, to complete melting. Stir until smooth. Drop bonbons in chocolate remove with spoon and place on a buttered wax paper. When dry, place in paper candy cups.

PEANUT BRITTLE

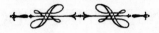

Ingredients:

2	cups	Sugar	2	Tbs	Butter
1	cup	Light corn syrup	2	Tbs	Vanilla extract
1	cup	Water	2	tsp	Baking soda
3	cups	Spanish peanuts	1	dash	Salt

Combine sugar, salt, syrup and water in large saucepan. Cook 15 minutes or longer on medium heat until mixture spins a thread or reaches 275°F on a candy thermometer. Stir occasionally. Add peanuts, cook 8 minutes longer and stir occasionally. Add butter and vanilla, and cook 2 minutes, watching closely. Sprinkle baking soda over top; stir 15 seconds. Immediately pour into buttered cookie sheet with sides. Cool, break into pieces.

PEANUT BUTTER FUDGE

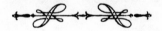

Ingredients:

14	oz	Sweetened condensed milk	3/4	cup	Creamy peanut butter
			10	oz	White chocolate chips
3/4	cup	Peanuts, chopped	1	tsp	Vanilla extract

Line 8-inch square pan with foil, extending foil over edges. Butter foil; set aside. In large saucepan, heat sweetened condensed milk and peanut butter over medium heat until mixture begins to boil, stirring constantly. Remove from heat. Stir in white chocolate until smooth. Immediately stir in peanuts and vanilla. Pour into prepared pan; spread evenly. Cool. Cut into squares and store in a covered container.

PEANUT BUTTER FUDGE II

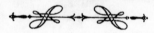

Ingredients:

14	oz	Sweetened condensed milk	2	cups	Peanut butter chips
			1	tsp	Vanilla extract
1	cup	Semisweet chocolate chips	1/2	cup	Butter

Line a 9x9 inch square pan with wax paper. In a medium sized saucepan, combine butter and sweetened condensed milk over medium heat. Whit butter has melted and blended away, add peanut butter chips, chocolate chips and vanilla. Stir constantly until chips have all melted and blended together. Pour the mixture into prepared pan and chill for 3-4 hours. Cut into squares when cool.

PEANUT BUTTER MARSHMALLOW FUDGE

Ingredients:

3	cups	Miniature marshmallows	1	cup	Peanuts
2	cups	White chocolate chips	2-1/2	cups	Sugar
2	cups	Peanut butter chips	1	cup	Peanut butter
1	cup	Evaporated milk	1	tsp	Vanilla extract

Butter a 9x13x2 inch pan. Coarsely chop peanuts. Combine the sugar and evaporated milk in a buttered 4-quart heavy saucepan. Cook on medium heat until it comes to a boil, stirring constantly. Keep cooking and stirring for about 5 minutes while at a rolling boil, until candy thermometer reaches 234ºF or until a small amount dropped from a spoon into ice water forms a soft ball. Remove from the heat. Stir in the marshmallows, white chocolate and peanut butter chips until melted. Beat in the peanut butter until mixture is smooth. Stir in the vanilla and nuts until evenly blended. Place in a prepared pan. Cool and cut into squares.

PECAN CARAMEL FUDGE

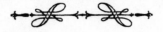

Ingredients:

7	oz	Marshmallow crème	2-1/2	cups	Sugar
24	each	Caramels, quartered	12	oz	Semisweet
3/4	cup	Toasted pecans			chocolate chips
1/3	cup	Butter, softened	1	tsp	Vanilla extract
5	oz	Evaporated milk			

Line a 9-inch square baking pan with foil; butter the foil with 2 teaspoons butter. Set aside. In a large heavy saucepan, combine milk, sugar and remaining butter. Cook over medium heat, stirring continuously, until sugar is dissolved. Bring to a rapid boil; boil for 5 minutes, stirring constantly. Remove from the heat; stir in chocolate chips and marshmallow crème until melted. Fold in caramels, toasted pecans and vanilla extract; mix well. Pour into prepared pan. Cool. Remove from pan and cut into 1-inch squares. Store at room temperature. Yields about 3 pounds.

PECAN CHOCOLATE CARAMELS

Ingredients:

1	cup	Milk chocolate chips	2	cups	Sugar
14	oz	Sweetened condensed milk	1	cup	Butter
1	cup	Light corn syrup	1	cup	Chopped pecans

Butter a 9x13 inch pan. Combine pecans and chocolate chips and spread evenly in the bottom of the greased pan. Set aside. In a heavy 2 quart saucepan over medium heat, combine sweetened condensed milk, microwave bowl, melt chocolate chips on high for 1-1/2 minutes in a microwave. Pour the peanut butter chips on top of the chocolate and melt for 1-1/2 minutes more. Stir chocolate chips and peanut butter chips together and then stir in peanuts. Drop by heaping spoonfuls onto a buttered non-stick cookie sheet, and let stand at room temp. Makes 40-60 pieces.

PEANUT CLUSTERS

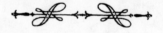

Ingredients:

12	oz	Chocolate chips	12	oz	Cocktail peanuts
12	oz	Peanut butter chips			

In a large microwave bowl, melt chocolate chips on high for 1-1/2 minutes in a microwave. Pour the peanut butter chips on top of the chocolate and melt for 1-1/2 minutes more. Stir chocolate chips and peanut butter chips together and then stir in peanuts. Drop by heaping spoonfuls onto a buttered non-stick cookie sheet, and let stand at room temp. Makes 40-60 pieces.

PECAN LOGS

Ingredients:

2	cups	Pecans, chopped	1	cup	Brown sugar
1/2	cup	Light corn syrup	1	cup	Cream
2	cups	Sugar			

In a heavy saucepan over medium heat, boil sugars, syrup and cream until the temperature reaches 236°F or until a drop from a spoon into ice water forms a soft ball. Cool to room temperature. Beat mixture with spoon until it holds its shape. Mixture will get much lighter in color. Pour out onto buttered breadboard. Knead until firm, keeping hands well buttered. Form into rolls about 4" long. Roll each in chopped pecans, wrap in waxed paper.

PECAN CARAMELS

Ingredients:

6	cups	Light cream, divided	4-1/4	cups	Sugar
2-1/4	cups	Light corn syrup	2	tsp	Vanilla extract
1	cup	Pecans, chopped			

Put sugar and 2 cups of the cream in heavy-bottomed 6-quart pan. Bring to a boil over low heat, stirring constantly, until mixture comes to a boil. If any sugar crystals are on side of pan, scrape them into the boiling mixture with a wet pastry brush. Add corn syrup. Cook, stirring, to the soft ball stage, 236°F on a candy thermometer. Add another 2 cups of cream; continue to cook and stir until the soft ball stage is reached again. Add remaining 2 cups cream; cook and stir until the soft ball stage is reached again. Each cooking stage takes about 20 to 25 minutes. The candy mixture becomes more caramel

in color as the cooking continues. The candy can burn more easily as the candy cools, so keep stirring. After the soft ball stage is reached the third time, remove from heat and add the vanilla and pecans. Pour into a well-buttered 9-by-13-inch pan, or two 9-inch square pans. Do not completely scrape the saucepan. Put scrapings in separate dish for samples. When the caramel has cooled completely, cut it into 1-inch pieces. Wrap each piece individually in small squares of waxed paper.

PECAN DIVINITY

Ingredients:

3	large	Egg whites	1/2	cup	Water
3	cups	Sugar	1/8	tsp	Cream of tartar
1	Tbs	Cornstarch	1/8	tsp	Salt
1/2	cup	Light corn syrup	1	tsp	Vanilla extract
1	cup	Pecans, chopped	Pecan halves for decoration		

Cover a work surface with greased wax paper for dropping the candy on later. In a large copper mixing bowl, beat the egg whites, salt and cream of tartar until they form and hold peaks. Set aside. In a heavy saucepan over medium-high heat, heat the sugar, corn syrup, cornstarch and water to the boiling point, stirring until the sugar is completely dissolved. Cover the pan of boiling syrup and cook for 2 or 3 minutes to allow the steam to wash down the crystals from the sides of the pan. Remove the lid and cook without stirring over

medium heat to 264F (hard ball stage). Pour the syrup slowly in a thin, steady stream over the egg whites, continuing to beat all the while. Do not scrape the saucepan. Add vanilla and beat until the divinity is satiny and holds stiff, glossy peaks. Mixture will be stiff. Add pecans and blend just enough to mix. Drop the candy by heaping spoonfuls onto waxed paper or a buttered cookie sheet. Press a pecan half into the top of each piece. Cool. Store in a tightly covered container.

PECAN PRALINES

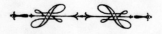

Ingredients:

2	cups	Light brown sugar	1/4	tsp	Cream of tartar
1	cup	Sugar	1/4	cup	Butter
1	cup	Heavy cream	1-1/2	tsp	Vanilla extract
1/2	tsp	Salt	2-1/2	cups	Pecan halves

Grease 3 cookie sheets. In a 2-quart heavy saucepan combine sugars, cream, salt, and cream of tartar and cook mixture over moderate heat, stirring until sugar is dissolved. Wash down sugar crystals clinging to side of pan with a pastry brush dipped in cold water. Boil mixture, undisturbed, over moderately high heat until the temperature reaches 236°F or until a drop from a spoon into ice water forms a soft ball. Remove pan from heat and cool mixture, undisturbed, until thermometer registers 220°F. Stir in butter and vanilla. Beat mixture until creamy and stir in pecan halves. Drop large spoonfuls of mixture quickly onto prepared baking sheets and let harden.

PEPPERMINT PATTIES

Ingredients:

7	cups	Confectioners' sugar	1/2	cup	Butter, softened
14	oz.	Sweetened condensed milk	1	tsp	Peppermint extract

Topping:

3	cups	Semisweet chocolate chips	3	Tbs	Solid shortening

Combine confectioners' sugar, sweetened condensed milk, softened butter and peppermint extract in a large bowl. Beat together until smooth. Tightly cover and refrigerate overnight. The next day, remove the mixture from the refrigerator, butter your hands and shape mixture into 1-1/4 inch balls. Flatten with the bottom of a glass to make patties. Place patties on a cookie sheet or jellyroll pan lined with wax paper and freeze patties for at least an hour. In a heavy medium-size saucepan, melt shortening and chocolate chips over low heat. Working with one dozen patties at a time, place each patty on a fork and dip into chocolate mixture. Transfer patties to a jellyroll pan lined with wax paper. Chill until chocolate hardens. Store in an airtight container in a refrigerator. Yields about 6 dozen peppermint patties

PERSIAN FUDGE

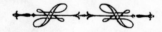

Ingredients:

14	oz	Sweetened condensed milk	1	cup	Pecans, chopped
			1/2	cup	Chopped raisins
1	cup	Sugar	1	Tbs	Vanilla extract
2	Tbs	Butter			

Combine sugar and condensed milk in heavy saucepan and cook over medium heat, stirring constantly, until sugars dissolve and mixture comes to a boil. Continue cooking to soft ball stage, 238-240°F on candy thermometer. Remove from heat and add butter, vanilla, nuts and raisins. Stir until well blended, spread on buttered platter or pan. Chill to set. Cut in squares when set and store in covered container.

PINEAPPLE CRÈME FUDGE

Ingredients:

1	cup	Pineapple pastry filling	16	oz	White chocolate chips
			7	oz	Marshmallow crème
2-1/2	cups	Sugar	1/4	tsp	Pineapple candy oil flavoring
1/2	cup	Butter			
2/3	cup	Evaporated milk	1	Tbs	Light corn syrup

Line a 13 x 9-inch pan with foil so that foil extends over sides of pan; butter foil. Butter the sides of a heavy 4-quart saucepan. Combine sugar, butter and milk in saucepan. Stirring constantly, cook over moderate heat until sugar is melted and mixture begins to boil. Add pineapple pastry filling and bring to boil again, stirring constantly. Continue boiling 5 minutes over medium heat, stirring constantly. Remove from heat and quickly add marshmallow crème and white chocolate chips; blend until smooth. Add pineapple candy oil and light corn syrup and blend. Pour into prepared pan. Cool to room temperature. Score fudge into 48 squares. Refrigerate until firm, cut into pieces.

PINK COCONUT SNOW

Ingredients:

1	cup	Coconut milk	6	cups.	Sugar
3	cups	Sweetened Flaked coconut	2-4	drops	Maraschino cherry juice

Combine sugar and coconut milk in heavy saucepan and cook over medium heat, stirring constantly, until sugars dissolve and mixture comes to a boil. Continue cooking to soft ball stage (238-240°F on candy thermometer), stirring occasionally to prevent scorching. Remove from stove and add coconut. Pour half of mixture into buttered jellyroll pan, spreading mixture evenly to the edges of the pan. Add a few drops of Maraschino cherry juice to the remaining mixture to give it a light pink color. Gently spread on top of the first half. Let set overnight. Cut into bars when cold.

PINK COCONUT CLOUDS

Ingredients:

3	large	Egg whites	1/4	tsp	Almond extract
1/4	tsp	Cream of tartar	1/2	cup	Sweetened coconut
2	cups	Confectioners sugar			

Beat egg whites and cream of tartar until frothy. Add sugar gradually, beating constantly until stiff peaks form. Add extract and 2-3 drop red food coloring. Fold in coconut. Drop by spoonfuls onto greased cookie sheet bake at 275° for 20-25 minutes. Cool on wire rack makes 4-5 dozen.

PISTACHIO CARDAMOM FUDGE

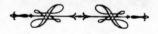

Ingredients:

4	cups	Sugar	4	Tbs	Light corn syrup
1-1/3	cup	Milk	1	tsp	Ground cardamom
1/2	tsp	Salt	1/2	cup	Chopped walnuts
4	Tbs	Butter	1/2	cup	Chopped pistachios

Butter a 9-inch square-baking dish Combine sugar, milk, salt and corn syrup in a buttered saucepan. Cook over medium heat, stirring constantly, until sugars dissolve and mixture comes to a boil. Cook to soft ball stage (240°F on candy thermometer), stirring occasionally to prevent scorching. Immediately remove from heat, add butter (do not stir) and cool to lukewarm (120°F). Add cardamom and beat vigorously until mixture is very thick and starts to lose its gloss. Quickly stir in nuts and spread into prepared baking dish. Sprinkle with additional chopped nuts if desired. Score while warm. When cool, use foil to lift candy out of pan. Cut into squares. Store leftovers covered in refrigerator.

PLANTATION PRALINES

Ingredients:

2	cups	Sugar	2	Tbs	Butter
1	tsp	Baking soda	2-1/3	cups	Pecan halves
1	cup	Buttermilk	1	dash	Salt

Butter the sides of a large heavy 4-quart pot. Combine sugar, soda, buttermilk and salt in buttered pot and, stirring and scraping bottom and sides of pot continuously, cook over medium heat for 5 minutes or until candy thermometer reaches 210°F. Add butter and continue to boil over medium heat, stirring and scraping bottom and sides, about 5 minutes or until the temperature reaches 236°F or until a drop from a spoon into ice water forms a soft ball. Remove from heat and allow to cool a few minutes, then beat until mixture just begins to thickens and lose its gloss. Stir in pecans, and immediately drop by tablespoons on waxed paper. Makes about two-dozen pralines.

PUMPKIN FUDGE

Ingredients:

2	cups	Sugar	1/2	cup	Evaporated milk
1/3	cup	Mashed pumpkin	1/4	cup	Butter
1/4	tsp	Cornstarch	1	cup	Chopped pecans
1/4	tsp	Pumpkin pie spice			

Cook sugar, pumpkin and milk until it forms a soft ball when dropped in cold water, or until mixture reaches 235°F on a candy thermometer. Add spice, butter and pecans. Beat until creamy. Pour into a buttered plate and cut into small squares

RAISIN & CHOCOLATE NUT CLUSTERS

Ingredients:

3	large	Egg whites	1-1/2	cups	Peanuts
1/4	tsp	Cream of tartar	1-1/2	cups	Raisins
3/4	cup	Confectioners' sugar	1-1/2	cups	Chocolate chips

Whip egg whites until stiff peaks form. Slowly whip in confectioners' sugar, a tablespoon or two at a time beating until stiff. Fold in raisins, peanuts and chocolate chips until just mixed. Drop mounded spoonfuls of mixture onto greased non-stick cookie sheet. Bake in preheated 375°F oven 10-12 minutes or until lightly browned. Cool. Makes about 4 dozen candies

RASPBERRY DIVINITY

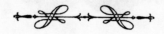

Ingredients:

1/2	cup	Sweetened coconut	3/4	cup	Water
3	oz	Raspberry gelatin	3	cups	Sugar
2	large	Egg whites	1	cup	Chopped pecans
3/4	cup	Light corn syrup			

Combine sugar, corn syrup and water. Bring to a boil, stirring constantly. Reduce heat and cook to hard ball stage 250-266°F. Combine beaten egg whites and gelatin - beat until mixture forms stiff peaks. Pour hot syrup slowly into egg whites, beating until candy loses gloss and holds shape. Fold in pecans and coconut (optional). Pour into greased 9-inch square pan. Top with additional chopped nuts and coconut, if desired.

RICH CHOCOLATE TRUFFLES

Ingredients:

12	oz	Semisweet chocolate chips	3	tsp	Cream
			3	large	Egg yolks
1	tsp	Brandy, raspberry or vanilla extract	3/4	cup	Butter

Grated chocolate, nonpareil decors or cocoa for coatings

In top of double boiler melt chocolate chips with cream. Beat until smooth. Continue beating the chocolate as the egg yolks are added, one at a time. Remove pan from double boiler and beat in butter, a few pieces at a time, until completely blended. Continue beating 2 or 3 more minutes. Add brandy or flavoring extracts as desired. Let chocolate sit, refrigerated, overnight. Next day, roll chilled mixture into one-inch balls; roll in either grated chocolate, nonpareil decors or cocoa to coat. Refrigerate. Serve in paper cups. Yields 2-3 dozen truffles.

ROCK CANDY

Ingredients:

5	cups	Sugar	1-2	drops	Food coloring
2	cups	Water			optional

Combine 5 cups of sugar, food coloring (if desired) and 2 cups of water in a heavy saucepan over medium heat. Stir until sugar dissolves, and then cook undisturbed until mixture reaches the hard ball stage or 250°F on a candy thermometer. Don't stir after sugar has dissolved. Pour the hot liquid into an eight-cup microwaveable measuring cup. Cover with aluminum foil. Poke wooden skewers through foil and push through until they touch the bottom. Cover the top, including the wooden skewers with more foil. Set aside for one week. After seven days, remove the foil and the skewers will be covered with sugar rock crystals.

ROCKY ROAD CLUSTERS

Ingredients:

3	cups	Semisweet chocolate chips	3	cups	Miniature marshmallows
14	oz	Sweetened condensed milk	2	cups	Cocktail peanuts
			1	cup	Raisins

In a large microwaveable bowl, melt chocolate chips on high for one minute. Stir chips until melted. Microwave an additional 20 seconds only if needed to completely melt chips. Stir in sweetened condensed milk until thoroughly blended and then microwave another 30 seconds. In a separate large mixing bowl, combine marshmallows, nuts and raisins. Stir chocolate mixture into raisin nut mixture and stir until well coated. Drop by heaping spoonfuls onto buttered wax paper-lined baking sheets; chill 2 hours or until firm. Store loosely covered in cool dry place.

ROCKY ROAD FUDGE

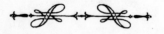

Ingredients:

Fudge:

10	oz	Evaporated milk	3	cups	Semisweet
2-3/4	cup	Sugar			chocolate chips
1/2	tsp	Salt	1	cup	Peanuts
4	cup	Miniature marshmallows	2	tsp	Vanilla extract

Topping:

| 1 | cup | Miniature marshmallows | 1 | cup | Peanuts |

Butter an 9x13x2-inch square pan, set aside. In a 4-quart heavy saucepan, combine evaporated milk, sugar and salt over low heat. Stirring constantly, bring mixture to a boil, and cook for 5 minutes.

Remove from heat and stir in marshmallows and chocolate chips, until both are melted. Fold in 1-cup peanuts and vanilla and pour into baking dish. Topping: Mix together marshmallows and 1-cup peanuts, and then sprinkle across surface of warm fudge. Press gently into surface of the fudge. Cool until firm and then cut into squares.

RUM-RAISIN FUDGE

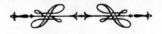

Ingredients:

Rum Raisin Mixture:

1-1/2	cup	Raisins	3	Tbs	Rum

Fudge:

3	cups	Sugar	3	Tbs	Light corn syrup
1/2	cup	Milk	3	Tbs	Rum
1/2	cup	Cream	3	Tbs	Butter

Mix raisins and rum; set aside overnight. The next day, butter an 8-inch square pan. Butter the sides of a heavy 4-quart saucepan. Cook remaining ingredients except butter in prepared 4-quart saucepan over medium heat, stirring constantly, until sugar is dissolved. Stirring occasionally, continue cooking until the temperature reaches 236°F or

until a drop from a spoon into ice water forms a soft ball. Remove from heat and quickly stir in butter. Cool mixture without stirring to 110°F. Beat vigorously and continuously with spoon or heavy electric mixer 5 to 10 minutes or until fudge thickens and loses its gloss. Stir in raisin-rum mixture until just mixed, and then pour into prepared pan. Allow to cool completely before cutting into squares.

SEAFOAM CANDY

Ingredients:

1-1/2	cups	Light brown sugar	1	Tbs	Vinegar
1-1/2	cups	Sugar	2	large	Egg whites
1	cups	Cold water	1/4	tsp	Salt
1/2	cups	Chopped nuts	1	tsp	Vanilla

In a buttered 4-quart saucepan, combine sugars, water and vinegar and cook over medium heat until the temperature reaches 236°F or until a drop from a spoon into ice water forms a soft ball. Remove from stove. Separately, beat egg whites and salt until stiff. When syrup has stopped bubbling, pour gradually into egg whites and beat well. When mixture begins to stiffen, add vanilla and nuts. Drop by teaspoons onto waxed paper. Makes 2 dozen.

SPONGE CANDY

Ingredients:

1	cup	Dark corn syrup	1	Tbs	Vinegar
1	cup	Sugar	1	Tbs	Baking soda

In a heavy pot, combine sugar, corn syrup, and vinegar. Cook over medium heat, stirring continuously until sugar is completely dissolved. Continue to stir and cook until a candy thermometer registers 300°F, or until a little of the mixture dropped in cold water forms a brittle thread. Remove from the heat and quickly stir in the baking soda. The entire mixture will bubble up. Stir well and then pour candy into a buttered cake pan. Candy will level by itself. Cool and break into pieces. Store candy in airtight container so it won't stick together.

SOUR CREAM CANDY

Ingredients:

3	cups	Dark brown sugar	1/4	cup	Butter
1	cup	Sour cream	1	tsp	Vanilla extract
1	pinch	Salt	1	cup	Chopped walnuts

Combine the sugar and cream and cook to 240°F (soft ball stage). Remove from heat and add a pinch of salt and the butter. Beat until mixture begins to grain. Stir in the vanilla and nut meats and pour into a buttered pan.

SUGAR & SPICE PECANS

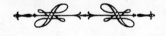

Ingredients:

1/2	cup	Sugar	1/2	tsp	Ginger
1/4	cup	Butter	1/2	tsp	Nutmeg
1	Tbs	Cinnamon	3	Tbs	Sugar
3	cup	Pecan halves			

In a 10-inch skillet, melt the butter. Stir in the pecans and 1/2 cup of sugar. Cook over medium heat, stirring continuously until the sugar thoroughly melts and the nuts brown. Stir in the spices and remaining sugar. Spread out on wax paper. Cool and break up the clusters into individual pecans. Store in a covered bowl.

SUGAR PLUMS

Ingredients:

3	Tbs	Orange liqueur	1/2	cup	Dried apricots
1/3	cup	Confectioners' sugar	1/2	cup	Golden raisins
1/2	cup	Chopped pecans	1/4	cup	Flaked coconut
1/2	cup	Prunes			

Finely chop the fruits and nuts. Add orange extract or liqueur; blend well. Shape mixture into 1-inch balls by rolling between palms of hands. Roll each ball in sugar. Store in airtight container in refrigerator between sheets of wax paper for up to 1 month.

SWISS MILK TOFFEE

Ingredients:

2	lbs	Sugar	1	Tbs	Butter
1	Tbs	Light corn syrup	1	tsp	Cornstarch
1	cup	Whole milk			

Grease a 9-inch square pan and set aside. Put all ingredients into buttered saucepan over medium heat, stir until sugar is melted, and then boil, stirring only occasionally, for about 20 minutes or until a small amount drop from a spoon in a glass of cold water forms a soft ball or until it registers 238°F on a candy thermometer. Remove from heat and beat for 10 or 15 minutes until mixture looses its gloss and becomes thick. Pour into prepared pan. Allow to cool about one hour and then cut into squares before candy completely hardens.

FIVE-MINUTE MICROWAVE MOCHA FUDGE

Ingredients:

1	lb	Confectioners' sugar	1/4	cup	Strong hot coffee
6	Tbs	Cocoa	1	Tbs	Vanilla extract
12	oz	Semisweet chocolate chips	1-1/2	cup	Butter
			1-1/2	cups	Chopped pecans
1/4	tsp	Salt			

Butter and line a 9x13x2-inch pan with wax paper. In a three quart microwaveable bowl, microwave chocolate chips and butter on high for 1-2 minutes, until chips begin to melt. Stir chips and butter until they are completely melted. Gradually beat in sugar, cocoa, salt, coffee and vanilla extract. Microwave mixture on high for an additional 1-2 minutes. Beat vigorously until smooth. Stir in nuts and then pour into pan; refrigerate for one hour, then cut into squares.

TIGER BUTTER

Ingredients:

3	cups	White chocolate chips
1/2	cup	Creamy peanut butter
1	cup	Semisweet chocolate chips

Melt white chocolate in microwaveable bowl on high for one minute. Stir until chocolate melts. If necessary, microwave in additional 15 second intervals and stir after each one. Only microwave until chocolate begins to melt, then stir to complete melting process. Stir in peanut butter and quickly spread mixture on wax paper lined jellyroll pan. Quickly melt chocolate chips in the same manner. Drizzle chocolate over peanut butter mixture in three long stripes about one half inch wide. Take a knife and swirl chocolate into the peanut butter mixture, being careful not to over mix. Refrigerate until firm, and then break into pieces.

TURKISH DELIGHT

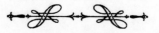

Ingredients:

2	cups	Sugar	4	Tbs	Powdered gelatin
3/4	cups	Water	1/2	cup	Hot water
1	cup	Lemon	1/2	cup	Confectioners' sugar
1	cup	Orange	1/4	cup	Cornstarch

Juice lemon and orange. Strain juice. Cut orange and lemon peels into strips. Set aside. Butter an 8-inch square pan. Set aside. In a heavy saucepan, dissolve sugar in 3/4 cup of the water over medium heat. Add the lemon and orange strips and juices. Bring mixture to a boil; simmer for 15 minutes. Soften gelatin by soaking it for 5 to 10 minutes in 1/2 cup of hot water. Add dissolved gelatin to sugar syrup mixture. Stir well and then return to medium heat to boil for about ten minutes, or until the syrup reaches the thread stage, about 280°F on a candy thermometer. Strain mixture into prepared pan. Let cure overnight at room temperature. Next day, cut the candy into 1-inch squares. Sift confectioners' sugar and cornstarch together into plastic bag; shake a few candies at a time in the bag to coat. Store candy in boxes with confectioners' sugar and cornstarch between each layer.

VANILLA COCONUT FUDGE

Ingredients:

2	cups	Sugar	1/2	cup	Evaporated milk
3	Tbs	Butter	1/2	cup	Coconut, sweetened
1/4	cup	White corn syrup	1/8	tsp	Salt
1	tsp	Vanilla extract			

Grease an 8-inch square pan; set aside. Combine sugar, corn syrup, evaporated milk, salt and butter in a saucepan. Cook over medium heat until the sugar is melted. Increase heat, and cook until mixture makes a soft ball in cold water. Cool 20 minutes; then beat until mixture loses its gloss. Beat in vanilla and coconut. Pour into pan. Allow to cool and then cut into squares. Store in covered container.

VASSAR FUDGE

Ingredients:

2	cup	Sugar	1	cup	Whipping cream
2	oz	Unsweetened chocolate, chopped	1	Tbs	Butter

Butter a 9-inch square pan and the sides of a heavy 2-quart saucepan. Combine sugar, coarsely chopped chocolate and cream in saucepan. Stirring constantly, cook over moderate heat until sugar and chocolate have melted. Continue cooking, stirring only occasionally to prevent sticking or burning, until mixture reaches 238°F or until a few drops tested in ice water form a soft ball. Remove from heat, stir in butter until melted. Allow to cool slightly and then beat until fudge begins to thicken and lose its gloss. Immediately spoon out onto buttered plate. Cut into squares before the fudge is absolutely firm.

VIRGINIA BROWN SUGAR FUDGE

Ingredients:

12	oz	Evaporated milk	2	cups	Brown sugar
1/2	cup	Butter	1	tsp	Vanilla extract
2	Tbs	Light corn syrup	2	cups	Pecans
2	cups	Sugar			

Butter a 9x13x2-inch pan and the sides of a heavy 4-quart saucepan. Combine milk, butter, corn syrup and sugars in saucepan. Stirring constantly, cook over moderate heat until sugar and chocolate have melted. Continue cooking, stirring only occasionally to prevent sticking or burning, until mixture reaches 234°F or until a few drops tested in ice water form a soft ball. Remove from heat, stir in vanilla and nuts. Allow to cool slightly, then stir vigorously until fudge begins to thicken and lose its gloss. Immediately spoon out onto buttered plate. Cut into squares before fudge hardens.

WALNUT BOURBON BALLS

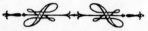

Ingredients:

2-1/2	cups	Finely crushed	1	cup	Minced walnuts
		vanilla wafers	2	tsp	Cocoa powder
1	cup	Confectioners' sugar	1/3	cup	Bourbon
3	tsp	Light corn syrup			

Coating:

1/2	cup	Confectioners' sugar	4	tsp	Cocoa

Mix together vanilla wafers, confectioners' sugar, nuts and cocoa. Add corn syrup, and bourbon. Mix well with hands and roll into 1-inch balls. Roll in confectioners' sugar and cocoa. Set aside in a cool place to ripen a couple of days.

WALNUT CREAMS

Ingredients:

3	cups	Sugar	1	cup	Walnuts, broken
1	cup	Light corn syrup	1	tsp	Vanilla extract
2	cups	Cream			

Butter a 9x13x2-inch pan and the sides of a heavy 4-quart saucepan. Place sugar, cream and syrup in a saucepan; boil briskly 15 minutes, stirring constantly. When small amount dropped in cold water forms a soft ball, remove from heat. Cool slightly. Beat until candy loses its gloss. Add nuts and vanilla; stir until it holds shape. Empty into buttered pan; mark in squares. Cut into pieces when cool.

WELLESLEY FUDGE

Ingredients:

2	cups	Sugar	8	oz	Miniature
2	oz	Unsweetened			marshmallows
		chocolate, chopped	1	Tbs	Butter
1	cup	Whipping cream			

Butter a 9-inch square pan and the sides of a heavy 2-quart saucepan. Combine sugar, coarsely chopped chocolate and cream in saucepan. Stirring constantly, cook over moderate heat until sugar and chocolate have melted. Continue cooking, stirring only occasionally to prevent sticking or burning, until mixture reaches 238°F or until a few drops tested in ice water form a soft ball. Remove from heat, stir in marshmallows and butter until melted. Allow to cool slightly and then beat until fudge begins to thicken and lose its gloss. Immediately spoon out onto buttered plate. Cut into squares before the fudge is absolutely firm. Store in covered container.

WHITE CHOCOLATE POPCORN

Ingredients:

1	lb	White chocolate	1	block	Paraffin
1	Tbs	Solid shortening	10	cups	Popped popcorn

Slowly melt white chocolate, shortening and paraffin in top of a double boiler over simmering water. Place popcorn in a large shallow bowl. Drizzle chocolate over popcorn; stir until  evenly coated. Spread the coated popcorn on wax paper and allow to cool. Break into small pieces. Store in an airtight container. Recipe is also good with semisweet chocolate in place of the white chocolate.

101

WHITE CHRISTMAS FUDGE

Ingredients:

18	oz	White chocolate chips	1/8	tsp	Salt
14	oz	Sweetened condensed milk	1/4	cup	Candied red cherries, halved
1-1/2	tsp	Vanilla extract	1/4	cup	Candied green cherries, halved
1	cup	Pecans, chopped			

Over low heat, melt chocolate chips with sweetened condensed milk, vanilla and salt. Stir until thoroughly blended. Remove from heat; stir in cherries and nuts. Spread into foil-lined 9-inch square pan. Chill 2 hours or until firm. Turn fudge onto cutting board; peel off foil and cut into squares. Store covered in refrigerator.

WHITE HOUSE FUDGE

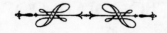

Ingredients:

1-2/3	cups	Evaporated milk	12	oz	German Chocolate
2	cups	Semisweet chocolate chips	2	cups	Marshmallow crème
			2	cups	Chopped pecans
4	cups	Sugar	1	tsp	Vanilla extract
2	Tbs	Butter			

Butter a 9x13-inch pan and the sides of a heavy 2-quart saucepan. Combine milk, butter, sugar and salt. Stirring constantly, cook over moderate heat bring to a vigorous boil, then reduce heat and simmer for 6 minutes. Meanwhile, place remaining ingredients (except nuts) in a mixing bowl. Pour boiling syrup over chocolate marshmallow mixture, beating until melted. Allow to cool slightly and then beat until fudge begins to thicken and lose its gloss. Stir in nuts. Immediately spoon out into buttered pan. Cut into squares when the fudge is absolutely firm.